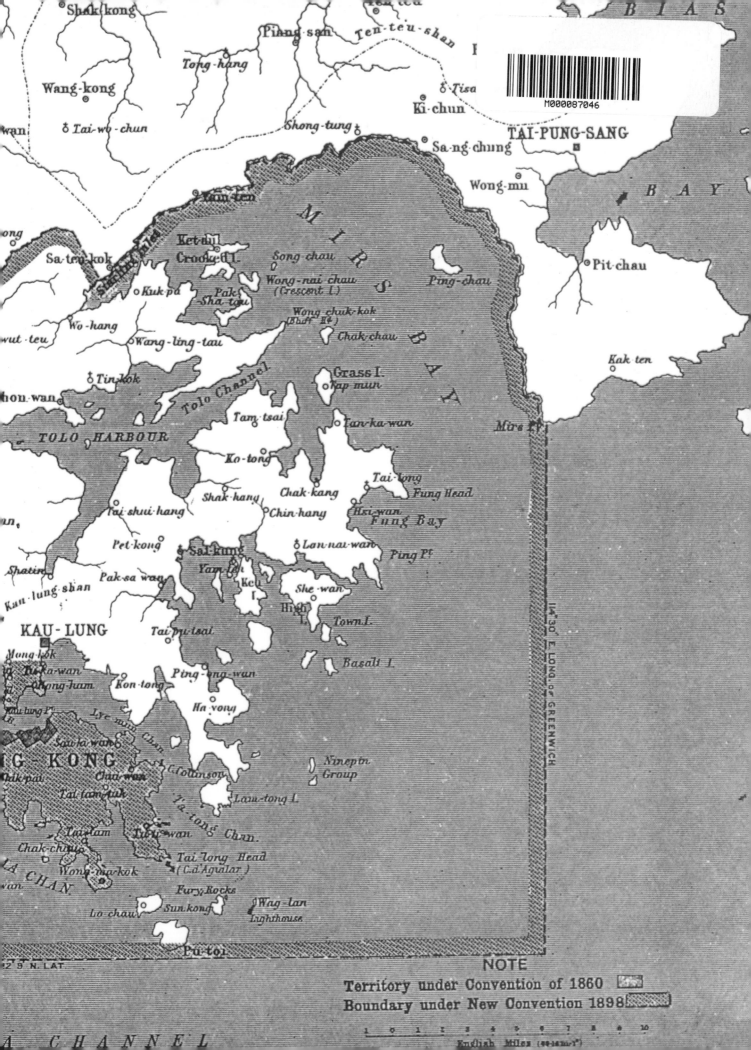

BIAS

Shak-kong

Tong-hang

Pang-san   Ten-teu-shan   I

Wang-kong

Tisa

Ki-chun   TAI-PUNG-SANG

Tai-wo-chun

Shong-tung   Sa-ng-chung

Wong-mu   BAY

MIRS

Yau-ten

Pit-chau

Ket-di   Crook-d I.   Song-chau   Ping-chau

Sa-teu-kok

Kuk-pa   Pak   Wong-nai-chau
Sha-tau   (Crescent I.)

Wo-hang   Wong-chuk-kok   Kak-ten
(Bluff Hd.)

wut-teu   Wang-ling-tau   Chak-chau   BAY

Tin-kok   Grass I.
Kap-mun

hou-wan   Tam-tsai   Tap-ka-wan   Mirs Pt.

TOLO HARBOUR   Ko-tong

Shak-hang   Chak-kang   Tai-long

Tai-shui-hang   Chin-hang   Hsi-wan   Fung Head

Pet-kong   Fung Bay

Sai-kung   Lan-nai-wan   Ping Pt.

Shatin   Yam-tan

Pak-sa-wan   Keu   She-wan

Kan-lung-shan   I.   High

KAU-LUNG   Tai-pu-tsai   Town I.

Mong-kok   Basalt I.

Ti-ka-wan   Kon-tong   Ping-ong-wan
Chong-ham

kau-lung Pt.   Ha-voug

Lye-mun   Chan.   Ninepin
Group

IG-KONG   Sau-ka-wan   C. Collinson

ak-pai   Chai-wan   Lam-tong I.

Tai-tam-tuk

A   Ta-tong Chan.

CHAN   Tai-tam   Tu-u-wan

Chak-chau   Tai Long Head
(C. d'Aguilar)

Wong-ma-kok

wan   Fury Rocks

Lo-chau   Sun-kong   Wag-lan
Lighthouse

Pu-toi

2°9 N. LAT   NOTE

Territory under Convention of 1860

Boundary under New Convention 1898

CHANNEL

1 0 1 2 3 4 5 6 7 8 9 10

English Miles (69·14m?=1°)

114°30′ E. LONG. or GREENWICH

THE HONG KONG STORY

the Hong Kong Story

Caroline Courtauld and May Holdsworth

With additional text by Simon Vickers

HONG KONG
OXFORD UNIVERSITY PRESS
OXFORD   NEW YORK
1997

Oxford University Press

Oxford New York
Athens Auckland Bangkok Bogota Bombay
Buenos Aires Calcutta Cape Town Dar es Salaam
Delhi Florence Hong Kong Istanbul Karachi
Kuala Lumpur Madras Madrid Melbourne
Mexico City Nairobi Paris Singapore
Taipei Tokyo Toronto Warsaw

and associated companies in
Berlin Ibadan

Oxford is a trade mark of Oxford University Press

First published 1997
This impression (lowest digit)
3 5 7 9 10 8 6 4 2

Published in the United States
by Oxford University Press, New York

© Oxford University Press 1997

British Library Cataloguing in Publication Data
available

Library of Congress Cataloging-in-Publication Data

Courtauld, Caroline.
The Hong Kong story / Caroline Courtauld and May Holdsworth, with
additional text by Simon Vickers.
p.   cm.
Includes bibliographical references and index.
ISBN 0-19-590353-6
1. Hong Kong—History. I. Holdsworth, May. II. Vickers, Simon, date.
III. Title.
DS796.H757C68 1997
951.25—dc21   97-19191
CIP

Printed in Hong Kong
Published by Oxford University Press (China) Ltd
18/F Warwick House, Taikoo Place, 979 King's Road,
Quarry Bay, Hong Kong

Acknowledgements

This is a companion book to the documentary film of the same title made by The Film Business Ltd, Hong Kong. The film was produced by Elaine Forsgate Marden, and directed by Libby Halliday. Our book could not have been written without their co-operation and help.

We owe an enormous debt of gratitude to numerous other people. Those who gave interviews and provided recollections are named in the book. Quoted comments in the text which are not attributed to printed sources have either been made to the authors in conversation, extracted from public speeches, or transcribed from interviews filmed for *The Hong Kong Story* documentary. Photographers and institutions that have lent illustrations are acknowledged under Picture Credits.

We should like to thank Chris Patten, who took time out of his extremely busy schedule in the final months of his governorship to write the last chapter of this book. Thanks are due to Simon Vickers, who collaborated with us on the writing of Chapters 4, 5, and 6. This book is also much enriched by the contributions of Richard Graham, Chan Sui-jeung, and Charles Jencks.

Although the sources of illustrations are listed separately at the back of the book, special mention must be made of Brian Pearce, Chan Chik, Yau Leung, Ingrid Morejohn, Carolyn Watts, Andrew Stables, and Greg Gerard, all of whom have been particularly generous in making their work available to us.

We are grateful to Julie Marchington, Natasha Edwards, and Anastasia Edwards for unstinting help with picture research; Penelope and Martyn Gregory, Margaret Lee of the Hongkong and Shanghai Bank, Elaine Ho and Matthew Hui of Jardine's, Kitty Lee of Hongkong Land, and Charlotte Havilland of Swire's for showing us numerous fascinating historical illustrations and allowing us to reproduce some of them; Eric Hotung, Diane T. Woo, David Clementi, Deanna Lee Rudgard, Adeline Yen Mah, David Tang, D. K. Newbigging, H. A. Crosby Forbes, John T. Hung, Alice King, Lady Youde, Millie Yung, Jeremy Waller, Carolin Weitzmann, Dr Victor Fung, Kim Salkeld, Edward Llewellyn, and Judy Green for information and support in various ways; our editors, Rachel Minford and Rebecca Lloyd; and, last but not least, Fanny Wong and Judy Yip for all-round assistance.

Foreword

by David Tang

I sailed for Athens as a boy of thirteen in 1967, the year of the Hong Kong riots. The departure was vivid: my great-grandmother, a third concubine, my grandmother, a first concubine, and my nanny, a spinster who first looked after my grandfather, all stood at the quay, looking up at my brother and me. Our new shirts and shorts, bought at the fashionable Shui Hing Department Store, had been their parting present to us. Like other passengers perched over the rails, we were holding on to an array of colourful streamers which still joined us to those below who had come to say good-bye. We did not quite know when we would see each other again.

As the small liner weighed anchor and slowly pulled away, the streamers became taut and I remember letting them go rather than letting them tear, as I did not want to break that fragile memento for the three women who had loomed so large in my childhood. I was also just grown up enough to be consciously lachrymose, and I tried to hold back the tears which had welled up in my eyes. I looked at my brother. He was doing the same.

As we navigated away from the Hong Kong harbour towards a shimmering dusk, I felt for the first time an acute tinge of sadness at leaving home. Being homesick became rather familiar to me at English boarding school a few months later, especially on those long Sunday evenings when I would most miss my great-grandmother and my grandmother and my nanny.

I was one of the first generations of children who left the shores of Hong Kong to study abroad. Thirty years later, scores of thousands must have similarly 'soaked themselves in salt water', as we Cantonese call it—although flying on VC-10s and 747s soon replaced the more romantic route I took of sailing through the mighty Indian Ocean, the Red Sea of Moses, the slender Suez Canal, and the amorous Mediterranean, taking in the Pyramids and the Acropolis *en passant*.

By whatever route, such temporary migrations of young Chinese have, to my mind, been a major factor in shaping Hong Kong and turning it from a mere backwater in the 1960s into the glittering cosmopolitan city of the 1990s. Just as those first China students who went abroad at the turn of the century returned to usher out the mighty Confucian imperial examination system in 1905, so the younger generation of Hong Kong Chinese brought home the Westernization which has been critical in transforming Hong Kong in the last three decades.

I suppose the most easily discernible change in that time has been the embourgeoisement of the Hong Kong Chinese. But that has come only with the final integration of the Chinese community which forms the vast majority of the population in Hong Kong. For years we Chinese didn't really live with or even near the British expatriates who more or less ran the colony. It wasn't until as recently as the early 1970s that the more prosperous Chinese (most of them having ridden high out of the shaky property market following the riots) started living up the hill on the island, and even on the Peak, which had been an almost exclusively white enclave. Such ascendancy was more than merely symbolic.

I remember Macdonnell Road at Mid-Levels first becoming rather fashionable, and my aunt, a quintessential product of the emerging bourgeoisie, moved into a brand new block there. One morning, she telephoned my mother (our home was still languishing in Kowloon at sea level) and complained that there were hawkers outside her block. My mother pretended to be horrified and asked my aunt why she had not got the Urban Services to chase them away. But of course my aunt had tried to do this but to no avail, whereupon my mother, trying to be helpful, suggested that my aunt write to a newspaper in order to spur the authorities into action. 'Don't be ridiculous, Rita,' my aunt exclaimed. 'If I did that, the whole of Hong Kong would know that there are hawkers on Macdonnell Road!'

So bourgeois consciousness arrived in Hong Kong and, I suppose, has entrenched itself further since. The wealthy will insist that they have every intention of staying in Hong Kong with its reversion of sovereignty to the motherland, whilst continuing to open an account or two at Coutts or Pictet, and seeking places for their children at Roedean or Eton. Most would also have British or foreign passports tucked away in their back pockets, conveniently hidden from their warming relationships with the New China News Agency or mainland cadres, now *de rigueur* in Hong Kong.

Nothing wrong with any of this of course, except that the roots of Hong Kong's success are now taken for granted, and too often it is forgotten, perhaps out of guilt or apologia, that British colonialism, nowadays weighed down with heavy political incorrectness, has been a substantial contributing factor. This is a pity because if ever anything good has come out of the British Empire and its colonialism, it is the shining paradigm of Hong Kong. Be that as it may, from now on Hong Kong will go forward on an alleged wave of Chinese patriotism. And soon the word 'colony', like the hawker below my aunt's apartment block, will be regarded with contempt.

It will indeed be fascinating to see what happens in another fifty years when Hong Kong truly reverts to China. After all, that maiden experience of 'one country–two systems' could not have applied to two more diametrically opposed systems. There will be a clash of a bourgeoisie underpinned by the best kind of capitalism, and a vicarious communist rule—for that is what is in store for Hong Kong and how that future unfolds only history will tell.

David Tang

Contents

A Note on the Romanization of Chinese Names

The majority of Chinese personal names in Hong Kong are romanized according to their Cantonese pronunciation; a small number are rendered differently. In all cases we have retained the spellings adopted by the people concerned. We have used the *pinyin* system of romanization, which is based on the Peking dialect, for mainland Chinese names, except for some place-names with familiar English forms such as Canton, Peking, and Yangtze.

A Note on Currencies

Several different currencies circulated in early colonial Hong Kong. As the mainland Chinese conducted their foreign trade predominantly in Spanish and Mexican silver dollars, the silver dollar was the most common currency in Hong Kong as well. The Spanish or Mexican dollar (equal in value) was worth about four shillings sterling in around 1840. Until 1862 Hong Kong government accounts were presented in sterling; thereafter the Hong Kong dollar, which was linked to the value of silver, was adopted. In 1935 the silver link was abandoned and the Hong Kong dollar was tied to sterling. Since 1981 it has been pegged to the United States dollar.

In this book, unless otherwise specified, sums of money are expressed in Hong Kong dollars.

CHAPTER 1

Concubine of Two Masters

Lord Palmerston

Hong Kong was colonized by the British not so much in a fit of absence of mind as in a spirit of compromise. When the territory became a part of Her Majesty Queen Victoria's dominions, it was regarded as a second-best acquisition. Its union to that great empire was a scrambled affair, the occasion of the first raising of the British flag, on 26 January 1841, not being dignified by any fanfare or much expense. Captain Belcher RN, who has given his name to a bustling street in today's Western district, did the honours, and afterwards the Queen's health was drunk.

As he made plain in a letter to Queen Victoria, Lord Palmerston, the Whig peer and Foreign Secretary, was 'greatly mortified and disappointed'. He would have preferred annexing Zhoushan or Ningbo on China's eastern seaboard. Expressing in no uncertain terms his exasperation with Captain Charles Elliot, representative of the British Crown in China, Palmerston wrote: 'You have disobeyed and neglected your instructions . . . you seem to have considered that my instructions were waste paper which you might treat with entire disregard, and that you were at full liberty to deal with the interests of your country according to your fancy.' Elliot, he felt, had been palmed off with 'a barren island with hardly a house on it. . . . Now it seems obvious that Hong Kong will not be a Mart of Trade.'

Though often characterized as a changeling of empire, or a 'natural child' of Victorian England and Qing China, Hong Kong may be more aptly compared to a less than favoured concubine. This was a secondary wife, moreover, who was received by the husband with some scepticism—as if he was rather unsure whether he had made a decent bargain. Her prospects were not fair: she had been given away by an uncaring parent casually enough, but she had not altogether extricated herself from paternal control either. After all, for some time after cession, Chinese residents of the British colony continued to be subject to Chinese laws, and Chinese customs duties still had to be paid on goods transhipped through Hong Kong. The

1

Qing-dynasty map of Sun On county which included Hong Kong

original terms of cession, Palmerston complained to Queen Victoria, 'had been coupled with a condition about the payment of duties, which would render that island not a possession of the British Crown, but . . . a settlement held by sufferance in the territory of the Crown of China'. Until the Treaty of Nanking was ratified, there was a chance that this barren island would be disavowed by the British government.

Even forty years into British colonial rule, the governor of the day, Sir George Bowen, was still recalling that 'the island of Hong Kong . . . when annexed to the British Empire in 1843 was merely a barren rock, inhabited only by a few fishermen and pirates.' This impression was probably fostered by Hong Kong's dramatic coastline, with its rugged granite boulders plunging into the sea and, rising behind, layers of sharp peaks covered by scrub. The few fishermen were certainly of no interest to the early British settlers.

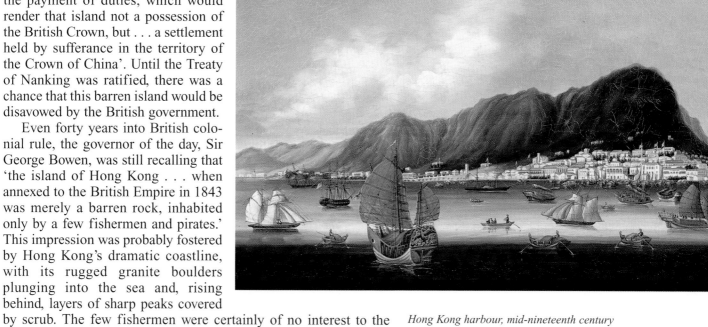

Hong Kong harbour, mid-nineteenth century

Early Days

The very first colonization of Hong Kong is thought to have taken place sometime around the second century BC. In 206 BC the Han Dynasty ousted the Qin and established their capital, Chang'an, in China's north-west. Consolidating the developments begun under the Qin, the Han made strides in agricultural methods which led to an increase in population and, in turn, fuelled the thrust of territorial expansion. Han rule extended to frontier regions such as Nan Yue in the south (corresponding to today's Guangdong province); Hong Kong was thus encompassed within the Chinese empire.

Of those early days the information is very sketchy; the group of islands was characterized by a wild landscape with the hills inhabited by tigers and snakes and a few aboriginal people thought to be of the Yao and Shan Lao tribes. (Some anthropologists believe these people were eventually pushed out by the Hans and settled in Vietnam.) Boat people fished the waters along the coast. The ancient Chinese name for barbarous tribes on the east of the empire was Yi, so the collection of uncouth aborigines in the remote coastal region came to be known as Nan Yi, Southern Barbarians. Later, the name Yi denoted foreigners in general.

Those who had settled along the shoreline, the Han histories tell us, wore their hair cut short, tattooed their bodies and lived in wooden structures on stilts. North- and west-facing beaches were the favourite sites, presumably because they were the most sheltered from the prevailing winds. Along these beaches crude tools have been unearthed, but little evidence of weapons for hunting, which inclined archaeologists to the belief that the settlers were

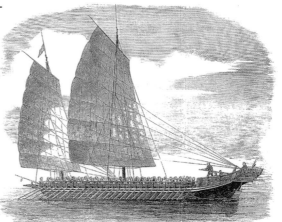

Pirate ship

3

Harvesting rice—some of the most prized rice was grown in the New Territories

Tanka woman with her baby

fisherfolk. The Han history texts also refer to the prevalence of pirates.

There is evidence too of a more sophisticated people, who were rice growers, in the lowlands of what is now the New Territories. We know something of the life of the small farming communities from the contents of the Lei Cheng Uk tomb, unearthed on the west side of Kowloon in 1955 when the site was being prepared for a new housing development. Among the relics found were pottery cooking pots and model houses, showing clearly that the culture of the Yellow River plain had reached this area as far back as the Eastern Han (AD 25–220).

By the Tang Dynasty (AD 618–907) Hong Kong waters, particularly in the Tolo Channel and around Lantau island, were producing the most prized pearls in the empire. Pearl fishing was a crude and dangerous affair. Each of the hapless divers (mostly a boat people called Tanka) was tied to a weighted rope which he would tug on when his breath ran out. Many a diver left it too late, and drowned before he could be pulled out of the water. Since it could not be pursued without a huge loss of life, the fishing was stopped for a brief period towards the end of the Tang. It was too lucrative to be given up entirely, however. After the industry was resumed, a military garrison of some 8,000 men was stationed at Tai Po, in part also to protect the small settlements from pirates.

During Tang times, China was visited by ships from India and as far afield as Arabia and Persia. Hong Kong's natural harbours provided a perfect anchorage for ships sailing between ports along the eastern coast and the Pearl River Delta. Uncertainty surrounds the derivation of the name of Hong Kong, which means 'fragrant harbour' in Cantonese; some say it refers to a stream on the island which supplied passing ships with sweet-smelling fresh water, and others that it comes from the incense which was made there at one time. The area remained thinly populated, however, although a military guard was stationed on the peninsula at Tuen Mun ('garrison entrance').

From the time of the Song Dynasty (960–1279) increasing numbers of migrants from the southern part of the Chinese Mainland began settling in Hong Kong; they were called Punti (from the Cantonese term meaning 'locals'). Hoklo people from further along the coast in Fujian also came, followed by the Hakka, and all of these immigrants carved out settlements for themselves. As the settlements were subject to the government authorities in Guangdong, they would be visited regularly from Canton by the magistrate-in-charge. One of these, Magistrate Tang Fu-hip, came in 1069 and was much captivated by the beauty of the countryside around the village

Tanka people

of Shum Tin (now Kam Tin, in the centre of today's New Territories). He was the first of the influential and extensive Tang clan who were to feature so prominently in the Hong Kong story.

When Magistrate Tang came to retire he moved his whole family to the area, as well as his ancestors' graves. He and his two sons and five grandsons were soon to become large and powerful landowners. Over the next two hundred years, four other clans arrived from inland China and made their presence felt—they were the Hau, Pang, Lin, and Man. These families, and in particular the Tangs, held the land rights of the New Territories and much of Hong Kong.

The ripples of China's dynastic changes reached Hong Kong twice during the turbulent expulsion of the Song Dynasty by the Mongols. As the Song court retreated from the northern invaders, a young daughter of the emperor found refuge at a loyalist encampment in the southern province of Guangxi. There are several versions of her story. One account attributes her deliverance to Tang Yuen-leung (the magistrate's grandson) who was a district officer in Guangxi at the time. At the end of his tour of duty Tang returned to his home in Kam Tin. By this time the princess had been accepted as part of the family though her identity was still unknown. Later she married one of Tang Yuen-leung's sons, Tang Wai-kap.

Many of today's New Territories villagers are descendants of the first settlers

Princely Hong

On 1 July 1997 the firm of Jardine, Matheson & Company will be exactly 165 years old. Though intertwined with the founding of Hong Kong through its early involvement in the opium trade, it is older than the colony itself. It has been called the 'Princely Hong' and 'Noble House' and, remarkably, has been run by the families of its founders up to the present day. Since the founders did not have children, the control of the company was passed on to their nephews and, through a female line on the Jardine side, to the Keswick family.

Its earliest incarnation was Magniac & Company. Charles Magniac, of French Huguenot extraction, had been a goldsmith in London. He went to Canton at a time when clocks, music boxes and mechanical knick-knacks were all the rage. His business was successful and soon he sent for his brother Hollingworth. When Hollingworth decided to retire, a partnership in the family firm was offered to a former East India Company ship's surgeon from Dumfriesshire—William Jardine. This partnership sowed the seed of what would develop into a considerable business empire.

Jardine in turn took on James Matheson as a partner. Matheson, a fellow Scot, also came to China via India. He had made a great deal of money in Canton, dealing in opium, and his business acumen matched that of Jardine's. The fortunes of the firm they founded—Jardine, Matheson & Company—would run parallel with the evolution of Hong Kong from a barren island to a trading, manufacturing, and financial centre of world stature.

It was through the triangular trade between Britain, India, and China that the Parsees first came into the picture and went on to found a community in Hong Kong. The Parsee merchants of Bombay were involved with the opium trade from early in the nineteenth century. One of them, Jamsetjee Jejeebhoy, befriended William Jardine; he and other Parsees formed the link between the source of the narcotic and the market for it.

Sir Jamsetjee Jejeebhoy

In 1129 the Song re-established a court at Hangzhou in southern China; the new emperor was the fugitive princess's nephew. It was only then that her whereabouts was discovered. At the happy family reunion the princess was granted the title Wong-koo, 'aunt of the emperor', and her husband, by then deceased, was ennobled with a posthumous title. Tang Yuen-leung's kindness was magnificently rewarded by the imperial grant to his descendants of one thousand *mu* (sixty-seven hectares) of land as well as tax-collecting rights.

The second time Hong Kong became an imperial haven was just before the final downfall of the Song Dynasty. Fleeing the Mongol army, the nine-year-old Song emperor Duanzong established a temporary court in Kowloon, in the shadow of a great rock overlooking the sea. Kowloon attributes its name to this emperor. On arrival he is alleged to have asked the name of the place. He was told it was Kowloon—'nine dragons'—after the peaks of the ridge of hills which lie behind it. Dragons, the traditional symbol of imperial majesty, are believed to inhabit mountain ranges. When the boy remarked he could see only eight, he was told that he, the emperor, was the ninth.

In 1277 the court made one final move across to the island of Lantau where, a few years later, the young pretender died. Later accounts tell of the boy's uncle who, despairing of any hope of a Song restoration, drowned himself and his nephew by walking into the sea with the child-emperor on his back.

Opium Wars and British Colonization

In the early sixteenth century, during the Ming Dynasty, when China herself had ceased to be interested in maritime exploration, European ships arrived at the southern coast. A Portuguese fleet reached Tuen Mun in 1514; there is a tale that the first Portuguese landed to bury his small son who had died at sea. It was a brief presence, however, as the foreigners were soon pushed back to Malacca by the commander-in-chief of the Guangdong naval forces.

China was withdrawing from the sea, but Portuguese sea power was in the ascendant, and the prospect of lucrative Eastern trade was too tempting to resist for long. In 1517 a flotilla led by Ferñao Peres d'Andrade and Tomaso Pirès sailed up the Pearl River to Canton, probably having stopped in Hong Kong to take on fresh water.

After some persuasion, the Chinese authorities gave the Portuguese the right to settle and operate a trading post in Macau. This was a privilege the Portuguese guarded jealously against their European rivals. A small squadron of English ships under the command of Captain Weddell dropped anchor at Macau in 1637, but the Portuguese, intent on keeping their monopoly of the China trade, resorted to duplicity. 'The jealous Portuguese intrigued against us,' an anonymous contemporary of Weddell's complained. Weddell was tricked by the Portuguese into handing over a quantity of silver to the Canton authorities, then found himself set upon by Chinese junks. Not only was the silver lost, but Weddell also had to apologize to the Canton officials and promise never to return to Chinese shores.

By the time English traders gained the upper hand over the Portuguese, the Ming had been overthrown, and the dynasty established by the Manchus, the Qing, was in power. It was a long time before the conquerors felt safe from Ming loyalist opposition. To sever contact between his subjects on the Mainland and the remnants of those loyalists in Taiwan, the Qing emperor Kangxi in 1661 ordered the people of the Guangdong and Fujian to move to fifty *li* (twenty-five kilometres) inland. In remote Peking this was no doubt regarded as a strategic decision; to the people of the littoral it was nothing short of a tragedy. A population upwards of 16,000 were moved and their farmland laid waste. Sun On county, which encompassed Hong Kong island, Kowloon and the hinterland including villages such as Kam Tin, remained desolate for years.

Life did not return to Kam Tin until 1669. When the restriction was lifted, China resumed maritime trade and four ports were opened to foreign shipping, Canton among them. There the Honourable East India Company—which held the monopoly on British trade with the East until 1833—established an agency house or 'factory' in 1699. Nevertheless China's reception of foreign traders was far from wholehearted. The court was accustomed to tribute-bearing missions coming to pay homage; rough and aggressive men like Weddell were quite another thing.

One of the hong merchants, Howqua

There was no holding back the commercial aspirations of Western traders, however. Finding conditions in Canton less than ideal, they ventured to the ports of Dinghai, Xiamen (Amoy) and Shanghai. By 1757 the emperor Qianlong felt the situation needed controlling. When a steep increase in the custom duties at the northern ports failed to deter the Westerners, he simply issued an edict prohibiting foreign trade at all Chinese ports except Canton.

The *modus operandi* for the Canton trade involved the traditional monopoly of the so-called hong merchants—thirteen in number at the time—who had imperial authority to conduct foreign trade ('hong', from *yang hang*, is the Cantonese term for a commercial firm). For their part these Chinese merchants paid huge contributions to the imperial treasury for the privilege. By all accounts they were respected; William Hunter, an American, said they were 'honorable and reliable in all their dealings, faithful to their contracts, and large-minded'. For a time organized into a guild, the Co-hong, these merchants supervised the trade transactions and stood security for the participants. They were landlords as well, col-

A tea warehouse

lecting rent from the thirteen foreign factories established along the Pearl River outside the city walls. The factory buildings were said to be comfortable, containing as they did spacious rooms behind verandas furnished with elegant bamboo *chaises-longues*.

In all other respects, however, the foreigners were highly constrained, as they had to abide by regulations imposed by the Chinese. From the Chinese point of view, trade was a privilege which foreigners should earn by their good conduct. At the top of the list of rules was the residence restriction: they could stay in Canton only during the trading season from October to January, when the winds

Opium ships

*Opium-smoking in China became widespread
by the early 1800s*

were favourable, and must otherwise return to Macau. Moreover, they were not allowed to move freely out of the factory compound; one walk a week in the company of an interpreter to the nearby garden was the full extent of their perambulations. Perhaps the greatest deprivation was the rule against female family members coming on shore. This rule made it abundantly clear that the Chinese allowed foreigners to stay in Canton only on sufferance.

Trade flourished despite the restrictions, though the prospects of making huge profits turned out initially to have been exaggerated. The problem was that the trade was overwhelmingly one-way: at home in Europe the demand for tea and silk seemed insatiable, but the Chinese appetite for British woollens, or ginseng and furs from the New World, was rather less voracious. More often than not the China-bound ships sailed with holds half empty, loaded only with the gold and silver needed to pay for Chinese goods. Unless the merchants could find commodities that the Chinese wanted in as great a quantity as the Europeans and Americans wanted tea and silk, there would be an increasingly unfavourable imbalance of trade.

Chan Sui-jeung, former Hong Kong civil servant and local historian, talking about his grandfather:

'As usual with rich Chinese in those days he was an opium addict, but he was one of the exceptional ones in the sense that he only had one wife and he did not have a single concubine.'

What tipped the scales was Indian opium. In 1773 the East India Company secured a monopoly on the production of opium which it sold at public auctions in Calcutta. The first shipment of the drug had arrived in Canton in 1729. Two hundred chests were landed (a chest was a measure for tea or opium, with a Bengal chest containing up to 160 pounds). Opium-smoking in China became widespread among all walks of life, from men and women of high social standing to the coolie in the street, and, by the turn of the century, there were nearly a million addicts in the country. Between 1810 and 1830 annual shipments soared from 5,000 chests to 23,000 chests. Magniac & Company alone imported 5,000 chests in 1830. Part of the traffic was handled by American firms which traded in both Indian and Turkish opium, though it was small compared with British imports. When the monopoly of the East India Company ended in 1833, the British trade in opium to Canton was turning over some twelve million Spanish dollars, while the American share was valued at about a quarter of a million. Soon Chinese tea and silk could no longer offset the massive imports of opium, and the flow of silver into China was reversed.

William Jardine

James Matheson

Opium, except for medicinal use, was banned in China by imperial decree in 1729 and banned absolutely in 1800. Since 'opium is the only ready money article sold in China,' as William Jardine—of the Canton merchant house Jardine, Matheson & Company—confided in a letter, it had to be smuggled in. The trade itself was thoroughly orchestrated. The East India Company refrained from carrying the drug in its own ships but licensed private traders to do so, with the Company reaping a portion of the profits. In fact massive profits were made at every turn. Normally an approaching vessel collected a permit off Macau and sailed up to Lingding (Lintin) island at the mouth of the Pearl River, where the illegal opium was offloaded on to floating stores. The legitimate cargo was carried on to Canton's Huangpu (Whampoa) docks through the narrow channel of the Pearl River Delta, known as Humen by the Chinese and the Bogue by Europeans. A pilot would board to guide the ship upstream. Once at the docks, the vessel was boarded by a hong merchant, an interpreter, and a comprador, and all the official procedures would be observed. Later, under cover of darkness, the Chinese merchants' own boats would collect the opium from the floating stores.

Quite apart from the effect of addiction on smokers, the drain of silver to pay for all this opium was precipitating a national economic crisis, and Emperor Daoguang (reigned 1821–50) realized that firm action had to be taken quickly. In 1838 he appointed a high-ranking official, Lin Zexu, as his envoy to deal with the problem. Commissioner Lin (as he came to be known) reached Canton in March of the following year. He immediately ordered the foreign traders to surrender all their opium and to sign a pledge guaranteeing that the smuggling would stop.

Over 21,000 chests of opium were delivered to Lin. Jardine, Matheson & Company—now run by Alexander Matheson, James's nephew—surrendered the most, followed by the rival firm Dent & Company, and the Parsee trader Heerjeebhoy Rustomjee. Lin arranged for the opium to be dumped in specially dug trenches by a river, then mixed with salt and lime and flushed out to sea. He

Emperor Daoguang

9

The Chuanbi Convention, signed by Charles Elliot

Lin Zexu, the emperor's envoy in Canton, solicited Queen Victoria's aid in suppressing the opium trade. Here are extracts from his letter:

'The wealth of China is used to profit the barbarians. . . . By what right do they in return use the poisonous drug to injure the Chinese people? . . . Suppose there were people from another country who carried opium for sale to England and seduced your people into buying and smoking it; certainly your honourable ruler would deeply hate it and be bitterly aroused.'

later noted in his journal that while the poison was being washed out to sea, he was saying a prayer to the spirit of the sea and advising 'the creatures of the water to move away for a time to avoid being contaminated'.

Lin's victory was shortlived, for no pledges were signed; instead, the foreign merchants called on support from home. A delegation led by William Jardine lobbied Palmerston, the Foreign Secretary. Lord Palmerston lent a sympathetic ear, and an expeditionary force from India was swiftly mobilized to blockade Canton. Meanwhile the British merchants in Canton withdrew to Macau.

William Gladstone, speaking in Parliament in 1840, said of the Opium War:

'a war more unjust in its origin, a war calculated in its progress to cover this country with permanent disgrace, I do not know and have not read of.'

He also noted privately:

'I am in dread of the judgement of God upon England for our national iniquity towards China.'

The specific trigger of the Opium War in 1839 was the accidental death of a Chinese from injuries sustained during a rowdy fight with British seamen on the Kowloon peninsula opposite Hong Kong island. Lin demanded justice, but Captain Charles Elliot, the British Superintendent of Trade, refused to allow British subjects to be tried by a Chinese court. The Commissioner retaliated by forcing the British community off Macau. Several hundred traders and their families had no alternative but to cram themselves into ships that lay off Hong Kong harbour, and there they sweltered through part of the month of August, watched by Chinese war junks and threatened with attack if they tried to make a landing. Naturally enough, tempers became rapidly frayed. In a skirmish between boats bringing provisions to the shipboard British on the one hand, and some Chinese armed junks on the other, the first shots of the Opium War were fired.

The British expeditionary fleet arrived the following June, blockaded Canton and turned northwards, taking Dinghai on the Zhoushan

Signing the Treaty of Nanking on the Cornwallis

islands in July before proceeding on to the Dagu Forts, which guarded the approach to the city of Tianjin. Up the river from Tianjin was Peking, so the expeditionary force was now dangerously close to the imperial capital. The emperor decided it was time to back down; his representative, Qishan, the governor-general of the region, suggested they all return to Canton to hammer out a settlement.

The settlement concluded then—though not without another show of strength by Charles Elliot—was the draft Chuanbi (Ch'uenpi) Convention. Its main terms provided for the cession of Hong Kong to Britain, though the conditions were 'clogged', as Palmerston later put it, with certain qualifications, one of which reserved the Chinese government's right to collect custom duties at Hong Kong. Somewhat prematurely, Elliot despatched Captain Belcher to plant the British flag on Hong Kong's western shore, and declared 'full security and protection to all British subjects and foreigners residing in and resorting to the island, so long as they shall continue to conform to the authority of Her Majesty's government.'

Palmerston, as we have seen, was unimpressed: Elliot had deplorably failed to drive a hard bargain. Both the British government and the Qing emperor repudiated the Chuanbi Convention, Elliot was recalled, and Sir Henry Pottinger was sent out with a fleet to bring the Chinese to heel. In the final stage of the war, Xiamen, Dinghai, and Ningbo fell to British gunboats. Then Shanghai and Zhenjiang were occupied. As the fleet closed in on Nanjing (Nanking), the Chinese offered to negotiate terms, and on 29 August 1842, the Treaty of Nanking was signed on the *Cornwallis*. It was formally ratified in Hong Kong ten months later.

This treaty, exposing the vulnerability of imperial China in the face of Western fire power, organization, and technology, was

Buddhist worshippers still throng the Man Mo Temple on Hong Kong island, which was established before British colonization

devastating for the Qing Dynasty. It is said that Emperor Daoguang could not bring himself to sign it immediately but paced his room for hours, occasionally muttering 'impossible' as he did so. At around three o'clock in the morning he managed to put his vermilion seal to the document. The treaty required China to pay twenty-one million silver dollars in indemnities; to allow Canton, Xiamen, Fuzhou, Ningbo, and Shanghai (the first of the so-called Treaty Ports) to be opened to foreign merchants and their families; and to cede the island of Hong Kong to Britain in perpetuity. Opium was not mentioned at all.

The Infant Colony

As long as uncertainty over the cession of Hong Kong lingered in the minds of those in government, the settlement could only develop haphazardly. Elliot went ahead anyway with several proclamations after 26 January 1841, one of which declared Hong Kong a free port. Then in May he announced a public auction of land. Fifty lots with frontage along a track running by the shore (later to become Queen's Road) were offered for sale. The best site was bought by one of the merchant houses, Dent & Company (or Dent's). James Matheson, as he informed a correspondent, 'secured three adjoining lots, and have built on the centre one, but contemplate establishing our chief seat of business elsewhere, on a point jutting out into the sea.' This was named East Point. As the historian Jack Beeching tartly commented: 'One man who immediately saw Hong Kong's potentialities was James Matheson: he moved the firm's headquarters there in January 1841 and began to build a large stone godown [warehouse], solid as a fortress. Whatever moral defects the opium dealers may have suffered under, they had an excellent grasp of practical reality.' The Navy naturally acquired a plot on the seafront; the Army settled behind, on the slopes of what became known as Victoria Peak.

The first Christian churches to be built were the Baptist Chapel, the Catholic Church of the Immaculate Conception, and the Union Chapel. An Anglican Church was not established until the Reverend Vincent Stanton arrived from Canton with his new bride. He preached his first sermon in Hong Kong on Christmas Day 1843, but it was another six years before St John's Church was completed. St John's Cathedral, as it now is, celebrates the 150th anniversary of the laying of its foundation stone in 1997. Places of worship also included a mosque and a Buddhist temple.

By the end of 1841 the fledgling free port was host to twenty-eight foreign merchants, with trade dominated by three firms—Dent's; Jardine, Matheson (or Jardine's for short); and Russell & Company from Boston, Massachusetts. The foreign merchants and Chinese did not mingle, the colonial tradition being to mark out separate quarters for the 'native' inhabitants. These areas, to the east and west of the European settlement of Queen's Town, were soon occupied by some 12,000 Chinese workers and tradesmen huddled in makeshift wooden or matshed huts cheek by jowl with cowsheds and pigsties. Away from Queen's Town—later named Victoria by Pottinger—the island was entirely rural, with villages nestled in the valleys. Lieutenant Thomas Bernard Collinson of the Royal Engineers, who drew the first contour of the island between 1843 and 1845, found that 'besides the town of Chek Chu [Stanley], there are ten villages and at least four hundred acres of well-cultivated ground.' The villages boasted 'a good supply of shops where bamboo hats, mats, sails, ropes and baskets; rice, fruit, vegetables, tobacco, earthenware and fireworks are all sold together.'

The Reverend G. N. Wright had observations on the ethnic make-up of the inhabitants: 'they were it seems both Cantonese and Hakkas. . . . The two groups appear to have occupied separate settlements in the island . . . though the population of the larger coastal fishing and market villages were mixed.' Another cleric, Issacher Roberts of the Hong Kong Mission, had in 1842 gone round and counted families in Chek Chu and found Punti, Hoklo, and Hakka numbering some 580 people.

Some of the villages were populated entirely by members of the same clan, descended from a founding ancestor. When the British arrived in 1841 the title deeds to much of the territory were held by the Tang clan, mentioned earlier. A Tang elder petitioned the magistrate of Sun On county thus: 'We inherited from our forefathers the taxable lands in the following places. . . . These areas have previously been leased to farmers Pang Shun-yau and Chow Ah-yow for cultivation. The situation has always been peaceful and quiet until they came and complained to us of forcible occupation of the lands around Kwan Tai Lo by English barbarians

British soldier painted in Zhoushan by a Chinese artist in the mid-nineteenth century

Albert Smith

whose ships were anchored in the neighbouring bay. These barbarians destroyed their crops to make way for roads and built huts on the unploughed fields. Knowing the fierce and violent nature of these barbarians, our tenant-farmers dared not negotiate with them. . . . We depend on the rents collected to pay our tax and support our families. Now that we have been robbed of our vital resources, where are we turn to for our livelihood?'

Soon, not only farmland but the tip of the Kowloon peninsula was being squatted on by the 'barbarians'. In principle all unused land in a colony was vested in the Crown. Nevertheless land rights were a complicated issue; unscrambling claims to land held before colonization even more so, especially when there were encroachments and unauthorized sales to contend with as well. The Tangs pressed for their claims to be upheld, though the *Friend of China*, an English-language paper launched by the American Baptist minister Lewis Shuck, was unsympathetic: 'As to his [Tang's] having been a Lord of this Isle, as well as of Tsim-shat-choy . . . we do not believe a word of it.' Eventually a modest compensation was paid to the tenant-farmers, but not to the Tang clan.

A Chinese supper in Hong Kong

Albert Smith, an entertainer from England, kept a diary, To China and Back, *between July and November 1858. In Hong Kong he was invited to a Chinese dinner:*

'This afternoon I went to a great Chinese dinner, given by A-chung, the comprador to the Peninsular and Oriental Company at Hong Kong, a man reported to be worth £30,000 or £40,000. . . . We went to A-chung's house, and up a ladder staircase, to the room where the comprador and two friends received us. They were jolly-looking, fat old gentlemen, dressed in white. . . .

We had, in succession, shark's fin: a stew of goose: tendons of deer: birds nest soup: turtle: ham (very good): fowls and quails: pigeons made up like faggots: fish sounds: small puddings of pork fat, as at the eating house: a soup of rose leaves, with a strong twang of garlic: and many unknown things. There were sixteen courses. . . . We ate as much as we could, for politeness, but soon knocked up.'

14

The early days were not easy for the new settlers either. On 21 July 1841, a typhoon lashed Hong Kong destroying much of the new construction, to be followed by a second hit less than a week later. Disease was rife. Dr Edward Cree, a Royal Navy surgeon, has left us a detailed account of his visits to Hong Kong. On 18 June 1841 he writes, 'Many men of the 18th Regiment have also died: many of the wounded from tetanus. Many a gallant fellow who escaped the field has succumbed to disease.' Then this note a few days later: 'Half our ship's company laid up with fever.' Sailing into Hong Kong again in May 1843, Cree reports: 'A great deal of sickness: disease is carrying off three men a day from the 55th Regiment at West Point Barracks. The sickness is attributed to turning up the new soil for building and road making and the quantity of disintegrating granite. There are no efficient drains made yet.'

Things had improved a little by 1850 when another visiting medic, Dr J. Bernacastle, recorded: 'The unhealthy reputation which Hong Kong had so justly acquired during the first years of our occupation . . . has now undergone an entire change. Proper drainage has been attended to.' But the good doctor found the heat unbearable: 'walking out in the sun quite impossible without an umbrella. . . . The summer in Victoria is very sultry and enervating, the thermometer often standing at 90 degrees in the shade.' He advocated 'flannel next to the skin', together with 'a generous diet and the moderate use of stimulants.'

The settlement of Victoria

Most of the original settlers in Hong Kong were farmers

Some of the community's health problems were self-inflicted. Brothels thrived where the male population, whether Chinese or Caucasian, far outnumbered that of the female. In 1845 there were only about 1,000 women compared with some 6,800 men living on shore. A law was passed in an effort to control prostitution, requiring registration of all prostitutes and designating certain areas for brothels, with separate districts for Chinese at the west end of the city and for Europeans at the east. Regular medical examinations were compulsory, and European girls usually complied though Chinese girls did not. Would-be prostitutes were expected to accompany their prospective brothel-keeper on a visit to the Registrar General to demonstrate that they were taking up the employment of their own free will. Nevertheless, Hong Kong could not totally wipe out venereal disease.

To the disgruntlement of the British government, the colony was turning out to be a costly acquisition even though it had come with an indemnity—one might say a 'dowry'—of twenty-one million silver dollars. In 1845 the budget showed a deficit of £49,000; the following year it was £36,000 in the red. The colony's main income was derived from land sales, rentals, and the opium trade. Contrary to expectations, however, business was far from good. The merchants were discovering to their chagrin that, having secured Hong Kong to facilitate trade, much of the shipping was actually bypassing the colony and going up the coast to ports opened as a result of the Treaty of Nanking. Instead of becoming a commercial emporium, Hong Kong was nothing more than a frontier town harbouring opium smugglers. For Dent's and Jardine's, the island was at least useful as a safe depot for the drug before it was transhipped up the

16

coast. However, ships that unloaded opium in Hong Kong still left it with empty holds.

Indeed, the high hopes for this new colony were fading. There was even talk of negotiating for its return to China, so deeply aggrieved did the merchants feel about the expenses they had incurred in moving there from Canton. Alexander Matheson did not mince his words: 'No! the devil of a dollar shall I lay out in Hong Kong except for the sake of a profitable investment.'

The gloomy mood was not helped by an outbreak of cholera in Western district, there being inadequate drinking water, little drainage and the citizenry's unspeakable habit of using rubbish bins as urinals. Immigration of Chinese from the Mainland increased dramatically as people fled the ravages of the Taiping rebellion (1851–64), putting tremendous strains on what public facilities there were. Suspicion and hostility festered between the Western and Chinese communities, and tensions in the city ran high. A number of measures to promote security, including a sort of curfew forbidding Chinese to go out into the public streets after nine o'clock in the evening without a lantern and written permission from their European employer, fuelled resentment.

Then, abruptly, all this discontent was swept away by an event of far greater concern.

There was no doubt that the merchants were on the coast to make money, and Matheson's dedication to profit was shared by them all. Anything that got in the way had to be eliminated. But with a complete disregard of the terms of the Treaty of Nanking, Canton officials continued to be obstructive. The frustrated merchants began clamouring for a revision of the treaty, and soon they found an ally in the Superintendent and Plenipotentiary in Canton, John Bowring, who was quite ready to provoke the Chinese Commissioner, Ye Minchen, to a showdown. Palmerston had already anticipated another war; in 1850 he wrote: 'I clearly see that the Time is fast coming when we shall be obliged to strike another Blow in China.'

The pretext for striking this blow was the arrest of the Chinese crew of a ship, the *Arrow*, while it was lying off Canton in the autumn of 1856. The Canton officers who made the arrest alleged that a notorious pirate was hiding on board. As the *Arrow* was owned by a Hong Kong Chinese and flying a British flag (although its registration in the Crown Colony had in fact expired), its seizure was promptly interpreted as an insult to Britain. Soon British gunboats were again seen sailing up towards Canton to engage in what became the second Opium War.

In Hong Kong, the anti-Chinese atmosphere was heightened by a case of mass poisoning. On 15 January 1857 some members of the foreign community were stricken after breakfast, having eaten bread later found to have been adulterated with arsenic. Cheong Ah Lum and his fellow bakers at the E Sing Bakery in Wan Chai were arrested but later acquitted for lack of evidence. As far as the hysterical foreigners were concerned, this was unnecessarily lenient and fair-minded; clearly they were victims of a sinister plot concocted with the help of those dastardly Chinese in Canton.

The second Opium War ended in 1858 with the signing of the Treaty of Tianjin (Tientsin), but not before the Chinese had burned down factories in Canton in reprisal, and British troops had taken Tianjin. In what was becoming a familiar pattern, another

Commissioner Ye Minchen

17

The E Sing Bakery

expedition and another flexing of muscle—including the sacking of the Summer Palace of Yuanmingyuan near Peking—were needed before final Chinese capitulation. The treaty ratification in 1860, known as the Convention of Peking, added the Kowloon peninsula and Stonecutters Island to Britain's Far Eastern possessions. They were to be held, like Hong Kong island, in perpetuity. Opium was not legalized, but its importation was permitted upon payment of a duty. Suddenly Hong Kong's future looked brighter.

Shamian

Shamian, as Richard Graham tells us, was a microcosm of the treaty-port world. Although Hong Kong itself was not a Treaty Port, its role as an entrepôt and China's window on the West was no different from that of Canton or Shanghai. In style it was very much the same, and from this evocative essay we may glean a flavour not only of expatriate life in nineteenth- and early twentieth-century Shamian, but also of all foreign enclaves on the China coast, including Hong Kong.

It is sometimes forgotten that several notable businesses and personalities in today's Hong Kong originated from Canton, and specifically from Shamian (pronounced in Cantonese to the foreign ear as 'Shameen'). Shamian, a British and French concession on the northern bank of the Pearl River in Canton, was born of one war and died during another, after a life of almost one hundred years.

The story starts in 1856, when the foreign factories in Canton were razed by the Chinese, and their some 300 foreign residents—predominantly British, American, and Parsee—retreated (as they had fifteen years earlier) to Hong Kong. Some, like Augustine Heard (who had established his own company after leaving Russell & Company), left for good. Others came back after an Anglo-French force captured Canton in 1857, and backed the plan of the acting British consul Harry Parkes to create an area, 1,000 by 300 feet, on the sand flats (or *shamian* in Mandarin) about half a mile upriver from the old factory site.

From an unpromising mixture of decrepit sheds on stilts, a stagnant swamp, and two forts, an embankment of granite filled with mud and sand was created and planted with trees. A canal was built on the northern side and two small bridges linked this artificial island with the city. This all took two years to create and cost the British and French governments 325,000 Mexican dollars (the French, invited to participate after their assistance during the invasion, contributed one-fifth of the money). Plots of

The burning of the foreign factories in Canton

Chinese and British officials on the occasion of the visit to Hong Kong of the chief Chinese negotiator at the Treaty of Nanking

land were sold to any foreigner, but not to Chinese, although a nominal ground rent was paid to the Chinese government. The French came slowly (and in the case of their first consul-general very reluctantly); the Anglican Church, Parsee property investors, and trading hongs on the British side rather faster. By the end of the 1860s Shamian was thriving.

As a centre of commerce Shamian was to be overtaken in the late 1800s by Shanghai, which grew rapidly after the Taiping Rebellion (1851–64), and it also fell behind Hong Kong in strategic and shipping importance. This reflected Canton's loss of its earlier monopoly position as China's window on the world. In large part this was because Canton's rivers did not allow for the deeper draughts of steamships and, later, propeller-driven vessels. The deep-water harbour of Hong Kong was to take much of what had been Canton's business. But for many years Shamian, first as a centre of tea exports and then of silk, was an important port in the China trade.

When the tea trade was overtaken by India and Ceylon in the late nineteenth century, the focus moved to silk, which became almost exclusively the commercial *raison d'être* of the French presence, exporting to Lyons and Zurich. Other commodities were also traded, however, and the Chinese Maritime Customs Service established detailed tariffs on all goods as early as 1861. These

delineated, for example, twenty-one kinds of cotton, twelve types of woollen goods, ten types of skins, and sixteen types of silk, as well as listing duties on kingfisher feathers, beeswax, camphor, and elephant tusks (whole and broken).

Some of the pre-eminent foreign trading houses that began in Canton still flourish. For the larger hongs—Jardine's, Swire's, the Hongkong and Shanghai Banking Corporation, the Chartered Bank and Banque de l'Indochine—an office in Canton was part of the treaty-port network, and all business there was conducted in Hong Kong dollars. Other firms that remain active in Hong Kong and China include Deacons, Arnhold Karberg, and Jebsen.

Shamian was a microcosm of the treaty-port world. By 1911 a community of some 320 foreigners and 1,100 Chinese lived in this small enviable corner of an overcrowded city, amongst banyan-shaded avenues, an English garden, and a French park; the Anglican Christ Church, a French Chapel, and a Masonic lodge; a club and a hotel. The community was watched over by a municipal council, complete with miniature police force and fire brigade.

There were few European wives in the early days, and even fewer single European girls. The female residents can be seen in late Victorian photographs in long

The Danish consulate at Shamian

skirts with croquet mallets, and later with amahs (Chinese maids), children, and perambulators in the gardens. In summer, wives and children would retreat to the relative cool of the Peak in Hong Kong, or to hill resorts further away like Guling (Kuliang).

All pre-war Western literature on the southern ports saw Shamian as a peaceful haven. It offered, besides, modern amenities. Already by Edwardian times it had septic tanks and a swimming-pool linked to the waterworks. But it also retained the formal dinner parties of an earlier era. In evening dress at tables 'adorned with full candelabra of Sheffield plate recovered from Canton pawnshops'—relics of an occupying Scottish foot regiment of the 1850s—the local taipans would be served soup, fish, brown entrée, white entrée, joint or game, a sweet, a savoury, nuts, and fruits. This left everyone too exhausted for more than 'mild bridge or other card games, polite conversation, and bed'. Less formal gatherings had boisterous party games, roulette, and visitors from Hong Kong to liven things up.

Somerset Maugham satirized the dull, anti-Chinese, and almost stagnant side of expatriate life in his *On a Chinese Screen* sketches. He spent six weeks, one resident recorded, with his 'male, fair-haired secretary . . . in the Victoria Hotel, with, I suspect, rats a many and bugs a few'. He drank martini, played bridge in the club, and

captured treaty-port life wickedly. Shamian inevitably thought Maugham ill-mannered when his book came out. Maugham also wrote the play *East of Suez* and a novel *The Painted Veil*—which cost his publishers £4,000 for libelling the Assistant Colonial Secretary of Hong Kong.

Between the wars life became more fun: there were house parties up the West River, picnics, golfing parties, and informal dances as well as St Andrew's and St George's Balls. There was never racing to match Hong Kong's or Shanghai's, but there were horses at Tongshan (east of the city), and early morning riding was a frequent part of life. Golf was played on land owned by the Kowloon–Canton Railway, also at Tongshan, though shunting lines and trains to and from Hong Kong did pose a hazard. Tennis was a key part of life in Shamian, and one of the more poignant letters in the archives of the Hongkong and Shanghai Banking Corporation is a Portuguese manager's apologetic request for a salary increase at the end of the Second World War, as he could no longer afford to buy tennis balls.

The remarkable thing about Shamian was how self-contained it was. Apart from Sir James ('Monkey') Jameson, British consul-general for twenty-one years, much of the rest of the community was largely cut off from the tumultuous events in twentieth-century China. A detachment of Baluchistan Foot Infantry was sent to

The Arnhold Karberg building in Shamian

Shamian around the time of the 1911 revolution that deposed the Manchu empire, and Punjabi troops were sent in the 1920s, but it was only the Shamian incident of 23 June 1925 that made the concession's inhabitants wake up to how vulnerable it, and they, were.

On that day, labour leaders in Canton led a demonstration to display solidarity with some Chinese students who had been killed by Sikh policemen, under the command of a British officer, during a rally in Shanghai. This anti-British demonstration marched close to Shamian's canal. Shots were fired by the French Bridge and thirty Chinese were killed. Whatever the reasons, whatever provocation claimed by both sides, this incident went down in Chinese history as a symbol of unacceptable foreign fire-power on Chinese soil, and hastened the demands by the Nationalist government for an end to extraterritoriality (which gave foreign residents of China immunity from Chinese laws). The more thoughtful of the foreign community knew that Shamian's treaty-port days were numbered. Only the Nationalist–Communist civil war and the Japanese invasion delayed Shamian's demise until the Second World War.

The last years of Shamian saw continuing decline. When Japanese bombs landed on Canton in 1937, Deacons opened an office in Hong Kong, as did Li & Fung, the Canton traders founded opposite Shamian's French Bridge. Foreign residents soon followed, on HMS *Moorhen*, to the downriver safety of Hong Kong, never imagining the Japanese would invade there too.

Extraterritoriality was renounced by Britain in 1943, and although the hongs returned after the war it was a different world. The silk industry had collapsed; the buildings on Shamian were occupied and took time to recover; and Nationalist bureaucracy was cumbersome. In the unsettled conditions of the late 1940s, much of the British consulate-general and other colonial buildings including Swire's offices were destroyed. Repairs were completed in time for the unexpected communist takeover. By the mid-1950s, after several years of harrassment and nationalization, the foreigners had gone, leaving behind nothing but their architecture on the sandbank of Shamian.

The buildings are still mostly there. The Victoria Hotel is now the Victory Hotel, and the British consulate-general has become the Guangdong Foreign Affairs Bureau. The churches have re-opened. The Customs Building still houses customs employees, and the Vietnamese police station of the French concession is still a police station.

Most of the present inhabitants of Canton know little of Shamian's past. They came after the war, and after the foreigners. You have to imagine the ghosts there for yourself—the French priests swimming on Sunday afternoons; and Costa de Moraes, the turn-of-the-century Portuguese consul in his cocked hat and handlebar moustache from ear to ear. Or Harry Parkes himself, the quintessential Victorian diplomat in treaty-port China, who became Minister to China and Japan, married a Keswick, and was remembered by a statue on the Bund in Shanghai—until the Japanese melted it down. There are other ghosts—the Vietnamese assassin who tried to murder the French governor-general of Indochina, the Parsee girls at school, and the salesmen in their grand offices at Arnhold Karberg. Or Henry Staples-Smith, bearded and serious, and six-times chairman of the municipal council. Looking to the river you might catch a glimpse of 'tiny painted-face girls behind silk draperies', or perhaps, later, the more brazen charms of the Russians on Shakee Street across the canal.

There are still some in Hong Kong who remember pre-war Shamian. For them the war led to the end of an era, but the beginning, in Hong Kong, of another.

— Richard Graham

One of the 'tiny painted-face girls'

CHAPTER 2

The Emporium Matures

Dent's house

Following the settlement of Kowloon, Hong Kong began stumbling towards fulfilling its destiny as the 'vast emporium of commerce and wealth' envisaged by Pottinger. Its transformation would not be immediate. The latest round of 'gunboat diplomacy' had secured ten more Treaty Ports for Western shipping; with that degree of competition, Hong Kong threatened to lapse into an even lesser trading station than it had been before. Of course it had its hongs, taipans ('big bosses' of the hongs), and compradors. It had all the trappings of a Victorian colony: Botanical Gardens; several churches and a number of gracious houses; a polo club, cricket club, jockey club, and of course the Hong Kong Club ('the paradise of the select and temple of colonial gentility', a civil servant of the day remarked). But it had yet to discover its identity and *métier*.

A visiting naval chaplain, Reverend McGhee, described the city in 1862 in a complimentary vein: 'As we steamed up the harbour the town of Victoria came into view, stretching along the foot of the mountain for a distance of more than four miles, if you begin at the Chinese town and measure up to Jardine's at East Point; then there are terraces rising over each other up the steep hillside, and built in the English style. Half way down the town, but high on the hill stands Government House, a handsome building. . . . Then the great mercantile establishments are chiefly near the water, close to the main wharf; on the left is Dent's house . . . while Jardine's is far away at the extreme end of town . . . the club-house, a convenient building, faces the Post Office in the centre of town in the Queen's Road . . . the right leads you to the Chinese town . . . but the chief families are on the side of the hill which is all tastefully planted.'

British enterprise and Chinese energy had indeed created a town where previously only a few straggling villages and some huts and matsheds existed. The sounds of construction (constant ever since)

The view west from East Point

Government House

were heard from within a year of British occupation; in the nineteenth century it was the bang of the stone mason's hammer. By the mid-1860s gas street lighting had been installed, a hospital, school, police station, and jail had been erected, a splendid clocktower some eighty feet high had been raised at the corner of Queen's Road and Pedder Street, and rich taipans' donations were being actively sought for the construction of a city hall.

Entrepôt

Coolies loading coal on to a steamer

A considerable influx of Chinese from the Mainland in search of employment in the colony had swelled the population; the acquisition of Kowloon boosted the number further, so that the whole population approached 122,000 in 1865, while it was only around seven

Western district in Hong Kong

to eight thousand in 1841. The figures fluctuated as there was constant movement of people between Hong Kong and the Mainland; there were particularly large numbers of transit passengers in the shipments of coolies—notably from Fujian and Guangdong—to the gold-fields of California and Australia. Greed and exploitation characterized this traffic, and the coolies were transported in the most inhumane conditions, being squeezed like so much cargo into squalid holds, ill-treated and frequently flogged through the voyage. The mortality rate was appallingly high. The colonial government, though concerned, bowed to pressure from the profiteers not to interfere. After all, the trade was valuable: coolie ships came to Hong Kong to be fitted and provisioned, and even hongs like Jardine's were involved as agents.

Lee Liang-yi, a native of Guangdong, was one of the lucky emigrants. Having managed to earn enough from gold-mining to return to Hong Kong, he settled down and started a family which would eventually translate his savings to great wealth through opium dealing. Other newcomers—free emigrants rather than indentured labourers—stayed to establish trades or to attach themselves to European companies or households. 'It was a curious sight', noted William Bernard in the late 1840s, 'to see the hundreds of Chinese labourers working upon the construction of our houses and roads, and flocking from all quarters to furnish us with supplies, and seeking their living by serving us in every way, at the very time when we

Chair coolies at work

were at war with their government, and carrying on hostile operations against their countrymen to the northward. At the same time, also, Chinese tailors and shoemakers were busy in their little shops making clothes for us, and Chinese stewards superintended our establishments, while Chinese servants (in their native costume, tails and all) were cheerfully waiting upon us at table.'

A list of occupations published in a government record, the *Hong Kong Blue Book* of 1872, reveals that there were more coolies, chair coolies, and servants than anything else. The next most common livelihood for the Chinese was carpentry. Hawkers were numerous too, followed by masons, barbers, stonecutters, and rattan workers.

As emigrants found work not only in America and Australia but also Malaya, Indonesia, and Indochina, an entrepôt trade sprang up in Hong Kong to cater to their hankering for products from home. In the reverse direction, exports from those distant shores entered China through Hong Kong. Nam Yeung Hong ('southern ocean companies') was the name given to the Chinese firms that traded with South-East Asia; Kam Shan Chong ('gold mountain firms') were those that supplied the Chinatowns of California. Nam Pak Hong ('north–south trading companies') traded across regions, handling a wide variety of commodities such as rice, tea, sugar, timber, dried seafood, silk, and rubber, as well as highly coveted medicinal and therapeutic items like ginseng, pearl powder (used to beautify the complexion and as a tranquillizer), rhinoceros horn, and musk. One of the first of the north–south trading companies was opened in around 1850 by a merchant from Chaozhou (Chiuchow), and a guild was inaugurated in 1868, establishing its headquarters in—where else?—Nam Pak Hong Street (now Bonham Strand West).

A receipt from a Nam Pak Hong issued in 1950

Close to where Captain Belcher raised the British flag in 1841, Bonham Strand was built over the first piece of reclamation carried out in Hong Kong. A fire in 1851 had destroyed more than 450 houses in the area. In the course of rebuilding, a creek was filled in using the rubble from the gutted houses. Clustered along Bonham Strand and providing the counterpoise to the colonial hongs, these 'native' trading houses generated considerable wealth for their owners.

Meanwhile the Western hongs were nurturing a new class of Chinese to work for them, men who were better educated and hard-headed like themselves. Essential as it was for the cultural divide to be bridged by at least a common language, it was not surprising that

26

the middleman role initially fell on Eurasians and Catholic mission-school-educated Macanese of Portuguese descent. On a December day in 1862, Ho Tung—later (as Sir Robert Hotung) to become Hong Kong's most famous Eurasian and certainly the richest—was born in a house off D'Aguilar Street on Hong Kong island. His father, said by some to be Belgian and by others to be British of Dutch descent, had nine children by his Chinese wife, but did not pass on his name.

The majority of foreign traders arrived in Hong Kong as young bachelors; there were also European sailors, soldiers, shopkeepers, and clerks. Like Alexander Matheson, the merchants would go home after their first tour of duty to marry (though in his case he returned to Hong Kong alone as his bride had unfortunately died in England). The 'fishing fleets' of husband-hunting English girls did not appear to come as far as Hong Kong; little wonder, then, that a Eurasian community began to emerge. Sir John Bowring, governor between 1854 and 1859, was vexed by the neglect of children born from interracial liaisons. Hotung and his siblings were more fortunate; although they grew up in acute poverty, they had a devoted mother, and, as with many Eurasian families who found colonial society more racially exclusive, they were brought up as Chinese. One Eurasian, Peter Hall, wrote about this many years later: 'Eurasians were . . . treated as out-casts, not wanted by anyone, as they were different, neither foreign nor native . . . one dressed in Chinese clothes, spoke Chinese, and if male may have worn a queue (pigtail) until 1911, then merged with the majority of the population to become for all intents and purposes "Chinese".'

Sir Robert Hotung in Western dress

Through the first few decades of the colony, government coffers continued to benefit from the opium trade on the principle that if the contraband could not be suppressed, then it might as well be taxed. When the import of opium was, for all practical purposes, legalized by the Treaty of Tianjin, a whole crop of problems over duty evasion arose.

This partly resulted from the details of the custom tariff set out in the Supplementary Treaty of the Bogue (1843) which, to the fury of British merchants, still placed restrictions on the freedom of the port of Hong Kong and effectively allowed the officials in Canton to keep control of all Chinese shipping calling at the British colony. The hongs chafed at this control and, to a large extent, ignored its restrictions. And there the affair rested until 1860 when trade in opium was legalized. Once again, it seemed that matters had not been arranged to the foreign traders' satisfaction. Or rather, the custom duties stipulated by the Treaty of Tianjin still threatened to erode their profits.

Hong Kong harbour with HMS Vittorio Emanuele, *a barrack ship housing British troops, in the foreground*

Opium smokers

This detailed description of opium smoking is from the memoirs of Osmond Tiffany, Jr., published in 1849 and called The Canton Chinese or An American's Sojourn in the Celestial Empire.

'The colour of opium is a dark opake brown when it is first in market, and before it is prepared for use. It is boiled down until it becomes about the consistency of current jelly, and when carried about the person it is put into little horn boxes, and kept perfectly tight. Those who smoke it are very guarded and careful, as far as lies in their power, not to let it be known, as it might subject them to disgrace and punishment.

The pipe used in smoking opium is of peculiar construction, differing entirely from the common tobacco pipes. It is formed of a straight, round piece of bamboo or ivory perforated through its length, till about two or three inches from the end, there is inserted the bowl which is in itself singular.

It is shaped like a covered cup, and has a very small hole in the centre of its top. The smoker, either to be as luxurious as possible, or knowing that he will not wish to move after inhaling the magic flavor of the drug, adopts a recumbent posture. His attendant is beside him with a little box of the "forbidden fruit," a lamp burning, and a needle about four inches long, terminating in a sharp point at one end, and at the other in a little flattened spatula.

The head of the debauchee is supported by a pillow, he puts the pipe to his mouth, and his attendant takes upon the flat end of the needle a modicum of opium about the size of a large pin's head. This he places upon the orifice of the bowl, fires it with the lamp, pushes it in with the sharp end of the needle, and the smoker inhales it all in one whiff, as it burns and changes into vapor. Old hands at the business retain the smoke, and let it slowly disperse and escape finally through the nostrils or swallow it. The effect is soon perceptible, but the victim takes six to twelve pipes, according to the length that he has gone in this fascinating dissipation.'

Opium had first to be shipped into China on vessels flying a foreign flag, and via a Treaty Port. On landing, a duty was levied by the Maritime Customs Service (first run by Horatio Nelson Lay and later by the vigorous Sir Robert Hart) which was responsible to Peking. Meanwhile the Chinese Commissioner at Canton continued to exact duty on the coastal trade carried by native vessels or junks. This system was an open invitation to tax evaders, and both Chinese and foreign merchants spared no exertion in their attempts to avoid paying. Opium smugglers either bypassed Treaty Ports, or arranged for the drug to be carried by Hong Kong-registered (and technically foreign) ships even though the shipowners were Chinese. The loss of revenue to the Chinese customs did not make for friendly relations across the Pearl River Delta. In 1867 the capture of a drug-running junk off Hong Kong by a Chinese customs cruiser precipitated a period of intensive surveillance of native vessels which was interpreted by the outraged hongs as a customs 'blockade' of the colony.

Hong Kong's fortunes, which had been lifted by the acquisition of Kowloon, now dipped, forcing many firms into

The mint in Hong Kong, first opened in 1866 and located in today's Causeway Bay. It produced coins of one dollar, fifty cents, ten cents, and five cents, but was closed down after only two years of operation

bankruptcy. The most spectacular failure was that of Dent & Company, one of the original and most influential China hongs, and a rival of Jardine's. Six of the eleven banks in the colony also shut their doors. Paradoxically, it was just before this series of financial collapses that the Hongkong and Shanghai Banking Corporation was founded in 1865. Unlike Dent & Company, which backed it, the bank managed to ride the storm of economic recession.

To deal with the economic crisis the governor, Sir Richard Macdonnell, put all unnecessary public works on hold. Various payments to the Colonial Office were withheld and a stamp duty was introduced, much to the annoyance of the business community who grumbled about 'over-regulation'. Macdonnell also borrowed $80,000 from the Hongkong and Shanghai Banking Corporation for the administration's essential housekeeping.

The founder of the bank, Thomas Sutherland, had something others lacked at the time—faith in Hong Kong. A Scot from Aberdeen, he was the Peninsular & Oriental Steam Navigation Company's agent in the colony. Besides establishing a bank, he lent his support to the formation of the Hong Kong & Whampoa Dock Company in 1863. In giving Hong Kong equal billing with Whampoa—the dock at Canton—the name of the new company reflected a recognition that the colony as a port was coming into its own at last. Not only that, it was an endorsement of a new commercial reality—from then on Hong Kong would no longer be just a smugglers' den, nor would the China coast be a mere appendage of British India.

29

Pioneers and Entrepreneurs

This new confidence and respectability pervaded Hong society too. British bankers and company directors went to their offices in Victoria with all the self-importance of financiers in the City of London. They wore their dark coats even in the blistering heat, but at least with the advent of the Peak Tramway in 1888 they could move up to the cooler air of 'their own special residential preserve amongst the clouds'. Pumped water and a police station added to the comfort and security of the lofty enclave. Sedan chairs were the preferred means of transport along the steep paths not reached by the funicular—except for the Indian Jew Emmanuel Rafael Belilios, chairman of the Hongkong and Shanghai Bank in 1881, who rode a

The Peak Tram

Andrew Choa, member of the Eurasian community:

'The Eurasian side comes from my mother. She was the granddaughter of that fellow Belilios. She never spoke a word of English although she looked very European, and some of our looks as children came from her. But she was 100 per cent Chinese in her behaviour, living patterns, and so on. . . . The kitchen was Chinese. The meals were entirely Chinese with the exception of breakfast: there you had a choice of either congee or bacon and eggs.'

---

camel to his mansion, the Eyrie. Rickshaws, imported from Japan, conveniently covered the short distances closer to ground level.

Life became more formal and the conventions more rigidly observed. There were lighter moments too, of course: the social round included dinners, balls, picnic parties, and amateur dramatics (originally held in a warehouse, later in a matshed called the Theatre Royal and, after 1869, at the new City Hall). With shops like A. S.

Amateur dramatics at the City Hall

Watson & Company, and Lane & Crawford, not to mention a cold storage company, the trappings of European entertaining were at hand. Since the expatriate society was dominated by the British, an inordinate amount of time was devoted to sport—from cricket and rowing to hunting and days at the races. On Sundays the expatriates went to church, and perhaps whiled away the long afternoons by reading in the library at the City Hall.

On Sundays this library could be used only by Europeans. This was a rule which shocked John Pope Hennessy when he assumed the governorship in 1877. With his liberal ideas, he was to offend the foreign community often during his five-year tenure. His grandson, writing many years later, tells us that the resentful traders and their wives stopped accepting invitations to Government House and did not bother to attend his leave-taking in 1882. Leaders of the local community, on the other hand, did turn up at the wharf; as his grandson explained, 'Sir John Pope Hennessy [was] the first Governor to initiate a liberal policy towards the Hong Kong Chinese . . . and to treat the native races as human beings with rights equal to those of the Europeans.'

There were now some highly educated Chinese. One such, Ng Choy, had eaten his dinners at Lincoln's Inn and been called to the

Early colonial life was enlivened by boat parties

The women and children of a wealthy Chinese household

A street in early colonial Hong Kong

Governor Hennessy

English bar; he was also, incidentally, a man of property like an increasing number of Chinese in Hong Kong. Without reference to London, Hennessy appointed Mr Ng to the Legislative Council as a replacement for the taipan, H. B. Gibb, who had returned home on leave. Faced with this *fait accompli* the Colonial Secretary agreed to the appointment, but only as a temporary one. Ng Choy resigned from the Legislative Council three years later, in 1883, moved to China, and became a high-ranking official of the imperial government, ending his career as the first Chinese Ambassador to the United States.

One of the arguments Hennessy advanced for promoting the equal treatment of the Chinese centred on the fact that they now owned a large amount of property, having spread their businesses beyond the borders of their quarters and infiltrated the bastion of European hongs—that is, the central section of Queen's Road and up the slopes behind it to Hollywood Road. While it was now permissible for Chinese and European businesses to mingle in physical proximity, however, residential areas were still segregated. Hotung was famously the first Chinese (strictly half-Chinese) to be allowed to have a home on the Peak.

That still lay in the future. In the year that Ng Choy became a member of the Legislative Council, Hotung joined Jardine's as a clerk. Brought up in a Chinese household, he had nevertheless benefited from the English teaching of Central School (later Queen's College) launched by the educationalist, Dr James Legge of the London Missionary Society. On completing his studies at the school, he sat the examination in Canton for entry to the imperial bureaucracy and successfully passed into the Maritime Customs Service. Two years later he resigned and began his career with Jardine's.

Hotung was the perfect comprador. Clinching his first major property deal—from which he received handsome commissions from both the buyer and the seller—at a relatively young age, he became a millionaire very quickly. He resigned from Jardine's at the turn of the century and vacated the comprador's seat to his younger brother Ho Fook. From then on he multiplied his assets through a variety of enterprises in Hong Kong, mainland China, and Britain. At one time he was a director of eighteen leading companies and the largest shareholder and chairman of the board of several of them. It was no wonder that he became the Grand Old Man of Hong Kong. This was a status enhanced by his appearance in later life, which was that of a silk-robed patriarch with a venerable white beard. He was honoured by the colonial government, by China (among his twenty-two decorations was a Third Class Order of Excellent Crop granted by President Yuan Shikai in 1914), and knighted by King George V

Compradors

As a class, compradors (*maiban* in Chinese) emerged when the more able local clerks in a foreign firm rose to the position of manager in charge of the Chinese staff and were invested with the authority to supervise dealings with businessmen from the Chinese community. Some language ability was the first requirement. A comprador was interpreter, broker, fixer, and accountant rolled into one. While he was paid a salary by his firm, he stood to earn considerable commissions by nosing out opportunities and giving play to his entrepreneurial flair. Sometimes he would be more than an employee: he could invest his own money in a transaction in partnership with his taipan. In this way he could become as rich as his patron.

Sir Robert Hotung in old age

in 1915. It was then that he adopted the English name, Robert, and changed his surname to Hotung. His two wives and one concubine provided him with ten children, and his nurse bore him a son. The Ho or Hotung dynasty thrives still, with tentacles in many spheres of contemporary life in Hong Kong and Macau, including real estate, the professions, politics and public service, and art patronage.

Sir Robert Hotung's vision was shared by another knight bachelor, Sir Catchick Paul Chater. The end of China's custom 'blockade' in 1885 found the original traders looking about them for more lucrative and less bothersome businesses than opium; a Jardine partner of the day wrote: 'The trade has altogether gone to the dogs . . . the firm now looks to opium only for freight charges, insurance and storage.' In India, the opium trade was being controlled by the Sassoon family, and Jardine's withdrew from it altogether. By the late 1880s the Princely Hong had extended its interests to textiles, railways, sugar refining, ice-making (their first cold storage operation being the forerunner of Hong Kong Dairy Farm), and docks. James Whittall, the taipan of Jardine's in the mid-1860s, was the first chairman of the Hong Kong & Whampoa Dock Company. Jardine's now had branch offices in China, Japan, Great Britain, and

Sir Paul Chater

33

the United States. Hong Kong itself, as we have noted, was acquiring a new confidence. There was 'a rush of life' about it; the hotels were filled with visitors, while milling about on Queen's Road Central were brokers of many nationalities, including 'Britishers, Germans, Anglo-Indians, Chinese from Canton, Armenians from Calcutta, Parsees from Bombay, and Jews from Baghdad'. This visiting commentator in the late 1880s went on to say that pinned to the Hong Kong Club walls were 'a dozen printed "Expresses", timed with the minute at which they were issued, and the mail and shipping noon and afternoon "extras" of the daily papers giving the latest news of shipping, cargoes, and auction sales.' The moment was ripe for Catchick Paul Chater to bring off the deal of the century.

Paul Chater was descended from a line of Armenian Christians in Calcutta with several generations of experience in the oriental trade. Arriving in Hong Kong in 1864, aged eighteen, he first worked for the Bank of Hindostan, China and Japan. No doubt this early exposure to finance stood him in good stead, for very shortly he was running his own bill and bullion business. From broking it was a short step to property investment. His eye must surely have rested speculatively on the milling crowds on Queen's Road and then lifted up towards the foreshore. What came to him then was nothing short of brilliant: waterfront reclamation was the only answer to the land shortage and congestion. Filled with an unshakeable sense of purpose, he made a lobbying trip to London to help his cause. Six days before permission for his praya [waterfront] reclamation scheme was granted, he formed a new partnership with James Johnstone Keswick, the taipan of Jardine's, to launch the Hongkong Land Investment and Agency Company, which was of course to profit enormously from the new reclamation. J. J. Keswick, shown in his portrait with a fearsomely bushy beard, was a Jardine descendant through his grandmother, who was the elder sister of Dr William Jardine, surgeon and Canton merchant. In time Hongkong Land, as the company is generally called, became the biggest landlord in the prime business district of Central.

Much fanfare surrounded the laying of the foundation stone for the reclamation in 1889. The new waterfront road was named after the Duke of Connaught, who laid the stone, and the old praya after Governor Des Voeux. Chater of course was awarded *his* road in between them.

Going the way of most rich men, Chater became a pillar of the community. He built himself a palace, Marble Hall, above Conduit Road in Mid-Levels; he was a Justice of the Peace and Legislative Councillor, and he lavished his money on good works. His grave

J. J. Keswick

Early mode of transport in Hong Kong

Anton Chekhov visited Hong Kong in 1890 and left this reflection:

'The first foreign port on my journey was Hong Kong. . . . I drove around in a rickshaw, i.e. borne by humans, bought all sorts of rubbish from the Chinese, and got indignant listening to my travel companions abusing the English for exploiting the natives. Thought I to myself, yes, the English exploit the Chinese, the Sepoys, and the Hindus, but they do give them roads, plumbing, and Christianity: you exploit them too, but what do you give them?'

(with that of Lady Chater's) in the cemetery at Happy Valley is maintained through a bequest to St John's Cathedral, one of the churches he patronized.

Chan Sui-jeung, former Hong Kong civil servant and local historian:

'Don't forget that before 1870 when the British took the 7.5 square miles of Kowloon, Tsim Sha Tsui was a village, a fishing village. Mody [a successful Parsee businessman and philanthropist] had already built a sort of dock there, and he had to send his workers over by boat. . . . Eventually, virtually as an afterthought, he said, "Why don't we make it into a commercial enterprise and make it a fare-collecting ferry?" And that was the beginning of the Star Ferry.'

The Lease

The 1890s were a troubled decade. Turmoil in China depressed trade as did the perennial hazards of piracy and typhoons. The government, having given a tremendous pay increase to its senior officials, was forced to undergo some belt-tightening, for the Colonial Office voted to raise the colony's contribution towards its military defence budget. In vain did the Legislative Council plead for leniency, arguing that not only had several items of capital expenditure been met from Hong Kong coffers, but the recent depreciation of silver against sterling would make the financial burden even more onerous. Their protestations fell on deaf ears and London doubled the contribution.

A temporary hospital ward filled with plague victims

To add to Hong Kong's troubles, in 1894 an epidemic of bubonic plague caused some 100,000 inhabitants (about half of the total Chinese population) to flee to China. More than ten years earlier, a medical inspector, Osbert Chadwick, had issued a warning: 'the sanitary conditions of Hong Kong are defective, and call for energetic remedial measures.' A particular problem was the unhygienic way in which sewage was disposed of, for buckets of it were daily tipped into cesspools and then removed by nightsoil collectors who sold it as manure. 'My report will show the necessity for strong and complete measures of sanitation,' Chadwick continued, 'without waiting for the necessity to be demonstrated by the irresistible logic of a severe epidemic.' The Tung Wah Hospital had since been founded, it was true, and would dispense traditional

The area around Jordan Road in Kowloon

medical treatment as well as attempt some health reforms. But public works on such vital facilities as sewerage and water supply had never managed to keep up with demand, and the health of the community was about to bear the brunt. During an exceptionally cold spell in January when, according to a contemporary account, 'the whole Peak down to four hundred and fifty feet above sea level was ice-bound for three days', the first cases of bubonic plague were diagnosed. As the heat returned, the number of fatalities soared, first in the teeming slums of Tai Ping Shan (the Chinese quarter on the west of the island), later spreading through the colony. In his annual report Governor William Robinson, who had lost his own wife to the plague, described the year as 'one of the saddest and most disastrous in the recorded history of Hong Kong'. The death toll was some 500. Hong Kong was declared an infected port and trade turned away.

Modest reforms came out of this tragedy, but the inevitably harsh measures taken to curb the plague alienated and inflamed the Chinese population. Volunteer soldiers working for the Sanitary Board would descend on infected areas, disinfect and whitewash the houses, remove the corpses, and bury them unceremoniously in lime. The contents of the dwellings were then burnt. The Chinese did not always understand that these methods, which took no account of traditional burial rites, were urgent and necessary.

Victoria Barracks, home to the Hong Kong Regiment

It was not the most propitious time to propose an extension of British rule, but that was precisely what happened. The move to acquire the hinterland of the Kowloon peninsula was led by the business community as much as by the colonial government; Sir Paul Chater was most firmly of the view that it was needed as a buffer zone to protect Kowloon and Victoria island. Their anxieties centred not on China but on other trading nations competing for domination there. These included Japan, already the victor of a war with China; Russia, which was seeking a port on the east; and France, then expanding her influence outwards from Indochina. Britain did not wish to be left out, but the Foreign Office flitted between various possibilities, at one time condemning Governor Robinson, who had been strongly in favour of extension, as 'a somewhat impulsive gentleman'. Finally Britain joined the other European powers in the scramble for concessions in China and claimed, in addition to Weihaiwei in north-east China, an extension of Kowloon's boundary.

The Chinese would not countenance another outright cession; they offered instead a ninety-nine-year lease on some 365 square miles of territory from 1 July 1898. There was a further complication. North of Boundary Street, the original limit of British territory ceded by the Treaty of Tianjin, was a Chinese customs post and military station. This was Kowloon City, and it was regarded by the

37

*Sir Robert Hotung (far left) with Governor Blake
and other prominent members of the community*

imperial government as inalienable. Britain duly conceded Chinese jurisdiction but the reservation was not observed in the end, so that the walled city became a no-man's-land, a lawless piece of Chinese domain within British Hong Kong. The British accepted the rest of the agreement—the Convention of Peking of 1898—with good grace.

Sir Henry Blake, the newly arrived governor, made the formal announcement in Hong Kong. It was not greeted with universal approval. In what was about to become the New Territories, the life of the Tangs and their fellow clans had been little disrupted by the colonization of Hong Kong and Kowloon, so it came as a shock to the elders to discover in 1898 that their villages were to be absorbed into British Hong Kong for the next ninety-nine years. 'The English barbarians are about to enter our boundaries and take over our land, and will cause us endless evil,' exclaimed the elder of the Tang clan. Raising a private army of some 2,000 men to repel the Hong Kong Regiment, the Tangs mounted an armed revolt. Fortunately for the harrassed colonial troops, the fighting soon fizzled out and they were even able to carry away as booty a pair of gates from the Tang walled village of Kat Hing Wai in Kam Tin. These handsome iron gates, which went with Governor Blake back to his house in Ireland, were finally returned to the village in 1925.

CHAPTER 3

Phoenix in the Fire

Typhoon wreckage, 1906

At the turn of the century China was in political disarray. The anti-foreign rebel group, the Boxers, were laying siege to the foreign legations in Peking. Under the Dowager Empress Cixi, the Qing Dynasty was struggling to bring itself back from the brink of collapse. Opium imports, foreign wars, the huge indemnities paid after defeat, internal rebellions, and the escalating costs of loans had all taken their toll, and the Chinese economy was in tatters. The control of much of it had in any case passed to foreigners: the imperial customs service, as we have seen, was run by Sir Robert Hart; Western hongs dominated transportation; and Jardine's, together with the Hongkong and Shanghai Bank, was about to launch a Chinese railway-building plan. Emperor Guangxu, Cixi's nephew, had lent his support to a plan to modernize China and save her from further dismemberment by the European powers, but the attempt at reform was foiled by the Dowager Empress. At this point we find one of the Tang clan serving as a doctor at the imperial court in Peking; a decade later his second wife was nursing Sun Yat-sen.

The Hong Kong administration busied itself with public works. Since the population had risen to over 325,000, improving infrastructure was an urgent priority. Reservoirs were planned, though the perennial problem of water shortage remained unresolved, and in 1901 was aggravated by a terrible drought when water had to be shipped to Victoria from the New Territories. Another severe bout of plague erupted that same year and, in an attempt to cull the rats, a reward of two cents for every rat killed was offered. The offer was promptly withdrawn when the remarkably high figure of 43,000 dead rats was handed in—most of them imported from China. Osbert Chadwick was recalled to make another assessment of the health situation. This time he was accompanied by a plague specialist, Dr Simpson. Their report became the basis of the Public Health Ordinance of 1903, but plague was to break out again none the less

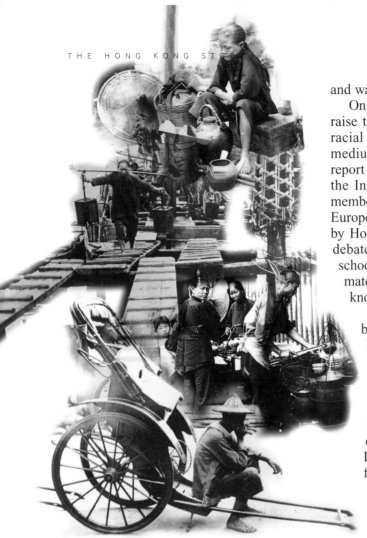

and was not brought under control until well into the century.

On the education front, Robert Hotung was active in helping to raise the standard of schools. This issue was never very far from racial considerations, as it invariably involved decisions on the medium of teaching, whether single-language or bilingual. The report of a committee convened by Governor Blake, which included the Inspector of Schools and Dr Ho Kai (a prominent Chinese member of the Legislative Council), recommended segregation of European and Chinese schoolchildren. A Kowloon school donated by Hotung to the government was unfortunately caught up in this debate. Though meant to be open to all races, it ended up as a school for British children only. Queen's College, Hotung's alma mater, continued to enrol boys of all nationalities (another well-known old boy was Sun Yat-sen).

The port of Hong Kong continued to expand and was to become the third largest in the world by 1910. Huge warehouses, several built by Chater, lined the Kowloon waterfront. In 1903 some 14,500 ships entered the harbour, 60 per cent more than ten years before. The bulk of this shipping was shared between Jardine's and Butterfield & Swire, another treaty-port hong. At the same time a mixture of industries was springing up: sugar refineries, flour-mills, cotton-mills, a cement works. The Central district took shape as Hongkong Land's reclamation progressed, and colonnaded buildings of four or five storeys rose on the recently named thoroughfares, Connaught, Chater, Des Voeux. The area marked out by these new buildings—a lopsided triangle of Queen's Road, Pedder Street and part of Ice House Street, and tapering towards Connaught Road—came to be called 'the flat-iron'. It still contains some of the most expensive office space in the world.

Butterfield & Swire was founded in Shanghai in 1866 initially to engage in shipping and trade. Jardine's already had a presence there. The two companies (through Jardine's Indo-China Steam Navigation Company and Butterfield & Swire's China Navigation Company) had long been rivals in China shipping, and in the late 1870s competed furiously for traffic rights on the Yangtze River.

A family group: Sir Robert Hotung, his sister-in-law Mrs Ho Kam-tong, and (standing) one of his sons, Ho Sai-lai

Both were now diversifying into other profitable fields in Hong Kong. Butterfield & Swire has since dropped 'Butterfield' from the company name; apparently one of the two original partners, Richard Butterfield, had been too grasping for John Swire's liking, and was made to retire.

One venture in which the traditional rivals were both involved was sugar. In this John Swire got the upper hand, having had the

40

Taikoo Dockyard staff and their families, c.1915. The expatriate staff at the dockyard were almost without exception Scottish

Jewish Merchant Dynasties

Governor Nathan

Apart from his support of the railway, Governor Sir Matthew Nathan is remembered for his youth (he was only forty-two when appointed), his opening up of Kowloon from what was formerly swampland, his promotion of education—especially technical training—and the fact that he was Jewish. While in Hong Kong, he was honorary president of the Ohel Leah Synagogue which stood then, as now, on Robinson Road. The synagogue was built in 1902 with a donation from Sir Jacob Sassoon. 'Sassoon' was an influential name on the China coast. Elias David (E. D.) Sassoon had arrived in Canton in 1845 from Bombay, where the Baghdad family had settled. He was one of eight sons of the patriarch, David Sassoon. By the time Hong Kong was ceded to the British, the Sassoons, prospering from the cotton and opium trade, were well on their way to becoming a merchant dynasty. Elias David and his brother soon set up in Shanghai and there the house of Sassoon built up a fortune not only in trade but also in shipping, property, and banking. It was E. D. Sassoon's son, Sir Jacob, who funded the synagogue and named it in honour of his mother Leah.

continued next page

good fortune to marry into a sugar-refining family (the company's Chinese name 'Taikoo' is still emblazoned on practically every packet of sugar sold in Hong Kong). By 1884, the Taikoo refinery was ready to process the raw sugar imported from the Philippines and the Dutch East Indies. As Taikoo's equipment was more modern than that of China Sugar (associated with Jardine's), the refinery went from strength to strength, and became, for a time, the largest in the world. It is hard to imagine now, as the residential and commercial skyscrapers soar ever higher, that the area stretching across today's Taikoo Shing and Quarry Bay also contained, besides the refinery, Swire's Taikoo Dockyard & Engineering Company, a sophisticated shipbuilding and repair operation.

This dockyard was not quite completed when Sir Matthew Nathan arrived as governor in 1904. Before giving his support to the colony's infrastructure, however, Nathan had first to turn his attention to stabilizing the currency, the value of which fluctuated according to the price of silver. He did this by demonetizing small silver coins and, sure enough, within two years the Hong Kong dollar's value against sterling rose from one shilling and seven pence to two shillings and three pence. Being an engineer by training, Nathan also took particular interest in a proposed railway line from Kowloon to Canton and beyond to Hankou (Hankow), but stayed only long enough to see the agreement signed before departing in 1907 for his posting to Natal. The railway line itself was completed from Kowloon up to the border with China in 1910.

In the early 1900s Governor Nathan would have found a small community—around 160—mostly of Sephardic Jews hailing from India and, before that, from the Middle East. One young man who came from Bombay to work for E. D. Sassoon & Company in 1880 was Eleazar Lawrence Kadoorie (later Sir Elly Kadoorie). It has been said of the Kadoories that they left Baghdad on camels and ended up in Hong Kong riding in Rolls Royces, and indeed Sir Elly Kadoorie & Sons is now an extensive business empire with a controlling interest in China Light and Power, and in Hongkong and Shanghai Hotels.

China Light and Power, as its name suggests, was originally a Canton company. Lord Kadoorie himself told the story, many years later, of its relocation to Hong Kong in 1901. 'In those days electricity was transmitted through overhead wires, and there was no way of preventing the theft of electricity by people who just hung other wires on to those particular mains . . . this stolen electricity went to the flower boat area of Canton, where the Chinese had all the brothels and—how shall we say—the jet set of those days lived. You could never get anybody to pay their bills. On the other side were the officials who, being officials, said why should they pay for electricity—it was not in the scheme of things. The result was that the company found it wasn't viable. So the chairman decided to sell the company to the Canton municipality. It was sold for a million Hong Kong dollars, which sum came back to Hong Kong and it was then that my father thought: why return it to the shareholders and wind up the company? Rather, let us start a company in Kowloon. And that is how China Light and Power came to Kowloon.'

The powerful Sassoon stable of companies at one time included the trading and engineering firm Arnhold Karberg (last encountered on Shamian in Chapter 1). Like several other foreign businesses in Canton, it relocated to Shanghai and later to Hong Kong. The controlling interest in Arnhold was acquired in 1957 by Maurice Green, father of its present chairman and main shareholder, Michael Green. Michael Green himself has spent most of his life on the China coast and now lives in Hong Kong. He has been chairman of the Trustees of the Jewish Community of Hong Kong since the death of Lord Kadoorie.

Governors Lugard and May

While the hongs were investing the fortunes they had already made from opium into legitimate businesses, the government was still deriving substantial revenue from the drug monopoly. For every ten Chinese in 1906, one was an opium smoker, and the annual revenue to the government from sales of its monopoly to the highest bidders was a hefty two million dollars around that time. Meanwhile mutterings against the evil trade were becoming louder. They were particularly strong in Britain, where the Society for the Suppression of

Old City Hall

the Opium Trade was agitating for the abolition of the monopoly and the closure of licensed smoking rooms or 'divans'. Public condemnation succeeded to some extent. In China, a decree issued in the name of Emperor Guangxu gave opium smokers until 1917 to drop the habit, and Britain agreed progressively to reduce opium exports from India until the trade would cease altogether by the same date. A gradual reduction of divans in Hong Kong did begin and no new licences were issued after 1910, although opium did not become illegal in Hong Kong until 1945. The colonial government compensated for the loss of revenue by taxing tobacco and alcohol, and by charging fees for the registration of motor vehicles.

The tottering Manchu imperial house of the Qing Dynasty finally collapsed in 1911, a few months before the boy emperor Puyi abdicated the throne. Sun Yat-sen, leader of the Nationalist Party, was then briefly the provisional president of the new Republic of China, but resigned in favour of the warlord, Yuan Shikai. One of the first actions undertaken by the new Nationalist government was to declare the import of opium from India illegal.

In the immediate aftermath of the revolution, however, all was joy and euphoria in Hong Kong. Many patriotic Chinese in the colony looked forward to a revival of China's fortunes under the new regime. Governor Sir Frederick Lugard, who had taken over from Nathan, noted much cheering and an outburst of nationalism among the Chinese population. A distinguished empire-builder with several years' colonial experience in Nigeria, Lugard moved decisively to defuse the incidences of local disturbance triggered by the Chinese revolution. His greatest contribution to Hong Kong was, however, in the sphere of education: he and his talented wife—a leading writer on imperial affairs—pushed hard for the foundation of a university in Hong Kong.

Lugard did not remain long enough to attend the opening of the University of Hong Kong in September 1912, and his place was taken by a new governor, Sir Henry May. Sir Henry arrived in Hong Kong on a hot July morning in 1912 straight into an attempted

Arrival of Governor May at Blake's Pier, 1912

assassination. Stepping ashore resplendent in ceremonial dress, he and his wife had just climbed into their gubernatorial sedan chairs when a shot rang out. It missed the governor but hit the chair of Lady May. Displaying true British phlegm, the governor instructed the welcoming party to proceed to the City Hall where he was to give his speech. Later he dismissed the would-be assassin as 'crazy', and the attempted murder as of no political significance whatsoever.

With considerable experience in the colony, having worked his way through the ranks from a cadet officer, May immediately sensed the changed atmosphere, not to mention the breakdown of law and order that continued to spill over from the disruptions in China. He took a strong line, introducing a deportation policy for undesirables and adding a provision for emergency powers to the statute book.

Instability and disorder on the Mainland did not deflect the foreign community of 20,000 expatriates from their usual pastimes. All manner of sporting activities could be enjoyed in the New

Lee Hysan

Although the opium trade was brought to an abrupt halt by momentous events in China in the early days of the twentieth century, the narcotic was clearly too lucrative to disappear from the streets overnight. As late as 1927 we hear of a libel case involving Pedro Lobo, the Opium Administrator for the government of Macau,

At the Hong Kong ferry pier the waterfront shop signs include one for an opium company

and the Yue Seng Company, which hitherto held the opium monopoly. Yue Seng was run by none other than Lee Hysan, son of Lee Liang-yi, the returnee from the Californian gold-mines mentioned in Chapter 2. Though undeniably a drug dealer on a massive scale, Lee Hysan did not conform to stereotype: born in Hawaii, he was not without education, for he had studied in California and attended Hong Kong's élite school—Queen's College—and even taught there. By his early forties he had bought land behind the Jardine's stronghold, East Point, which would blossom into Lee Gardens and one of the busiest and most valuable blocks of real estate in Hong Kong.

Lee Hysan did not live to see it. One day in late April 1928, on Wellington Street in the Central business district, within sight of a club he regularly patronized, Lee was shot three times. His murderer, thought to be connected with the dark and criminal world of opium dealing, was never found. Packets of prepared opium continued to be sold in licensed shops in Hong Kong until the Second World War.

Label on a packet of opium sold in Hong Kong

Blake's Pier

Territories, now accessible by train. There was golf at Fanling, with a break for tiffin served in a matshed beside the ninth green. Or a picnic party could sail from the newly constructed Blake's Pier to some idyllic beach. Governor May, a keen fisherman, saw to it that the reservoirs were amply stocked. To welcome in the new year in 1914 party guests arrived at the Kingsclere Hotel on Hong Kong island in 'costumes both costly and magnificent', according to the *South China Morning Post*. Less socially distinguished revellers attended balls at the Taikoo Dockyard or the Hong Kong & Whampoa Dock in Kowloon. For visitors from the Treaty Ports there were now several hotels to choose from: the Hong Kong Hotel, for example, offered 'large, airy rooms, electric light, lifts and fans . . . bedrooms with European bath and lavatory attached. Perfect sanitation.' Other typically English preoccupations included racing at Happy Valley on the small stocky ponies from China, and hunting

From the album of an expatriate who served in Hong Kong

George Wright Nooth, former Assistant Commissioner of Police:

'Well, the businessmen in Hong Kong did most of their business in the morning and dictated their letters. Then they went off to the Hong Kong Club and had several gin and tonics, and afterwards they would lie in long deck chairs, rattan chairs, on the veranda, sleep it off and go back in the afternoon to sign all their letters. . . . So life was not altogether bad.'

in the New Territories. Wild pig, snipe, and even tiger were out there to be shot. The Fanling Hunt, particularly its New Year's Day meet, and the Peninsula Hotel hunt ball remained popular for years.

This gaiety was cut short by the outbreak of war in Europe. Many British residents of Hong Kong left for the battlefields, while those who stayed set up the Hong Kong Volunteers. As would be seen in later years, the colony was generous with aid: huge private donations were made to the war effort, including the gift of two planes by Hotung. Conscription was introduced during the final stages of the war. All this provoked some soul-searching by the colonists: might not Hong Kong, which could marshall such tremendous support for the sovereign power, now be given some say in its own affairs? A petition proposing a change in the constitutional arrangements to include an elected majority in the Legislative Council was, however, turned down by England's Secretary of State on the grounds that it was not an appropriate time for such reform.

When Armistice was declared, Governor May was taking a respite from his duties in Canada. He never returned to Hong Kong. Meanwhile, the colony celebrated the end of the First World War in fine style, with parades and fireworks, and buildings in Central were spectacularly decked in bunting.

A more sober prospect was the shortage of staples and the runaway inflation. Food prices had rocketed; with the scarcity of imports the foreign community began to eat rice, and this in turn drove the price up in the market by a hefty 155 per cent. When aggrieved Chinese workers' demands for a pay rise were ignored by their employers, strikes were called. The first group of strikers operated under the Chinese Engineering Institute and the second was represented by the Seamen's Union, whose lawyer was Man-kam Lo, a notable Eurasian in Hong Kong and Sir Robert Hotung's son-in-law. His wedding to Sir Robert's eldest daughter, Victoria Jubilee, had been a landmark social event, attended by no less a personage than the governor, Sir Henry May.

The wedding was held in Idlewild, the Hotung house on Seymour Road in Mid-Levels. Hotung also owned houses on the Peak, an area that, since the passing of the Peak Reservation Ordinance of 1904,

Peace celebrations in Hong Kong, 1919

The Government House ballroom, decked out for the celebrations to mark the end of World War I

THE HONG KONG STORY

A salon in the Hotung house on the Peak

was effectively barred to the Chinese. Except for Chinese domestic staff, which in an upper middle-class household would have numbered around twenty—a dozen maidservants and several male houseboys and gardeners— Hotung was the only non-European to live on the Peak before 1945. There were chauffeurs as well, though the Hotung children rode donkeys down to the Peak Tram to catch the ferry across to Kowloon for school. A son of Sir Robert's remembers vividly the segregation in practice before the Second World War. The Hotung nanny (English, of course) was not allowed by the neighbours to bring her charges to play with their children. Here on the Peak was a 'little England', where life in winter was punctuated by long damp walks with the dogs, followed by a cup of tea and freshly baked crumpets in front of the fire. In the summer months, a game of tennis or croquet on the neatly trimmed lawn might be played.

Petty social distinctions were very marked in the inter-war years. Shanghai, rapidly developing as the more important port for foreign business, had none of Hong Kong's colonial snobbery. Speaking to a British journalist, Lord Kadoorie put the difference in a nutshell: 'Shanghai was international with people who had an international outlook. Hong Kong was very British. Who were the British? They were small shopkeepers in their mentality. It was a nice quiet little place. . . . If Shanghai was London then Hong Kong was Hastings.'

None the less, at least the racial chasm in business was narrowing. 'The Chinese are excluded from no department of commercial activity in Hong Kong,' Robert Hotung said. 'Chinese-capitalized, Chinese-managed, and Chinese-staffed joint stock companies doing business in fire, marine and life insurance, shipping, land and estate business, and shipbuilding and repairing, are no longer isolated instances of native enterprises.'

Li & Fung was such a company. Financed solely with Chinese capital, it opened for business, as we have seen, opposite Shamian's French Bridge in Canton in 1906, first trading in porcelain. But those celebrating crowds observed by Governor Lugard, whose firecrackers had added to the commotion, might well have been customers of Li & Fung, since the company soon had a profitable line in fireworks of all kinds.

In those days it was customary in China, as the Li & Fung company history explains, for deals to be made by 'gentlemen's agreement'—no documents were signed, nor contracts exchanged. Face-to-face negotiations often took place in select brothels known as 'singsong houses'. The merchants would begin by rolling down the long sleeves of their traditional gowns and, with hands joined under

A residential street in Mid-Levels

46

cover of the voluminous cuffs, their pressing fingers would do the haggling. The prices and quantities thus agreed were binding, and scrupulously honoured. However, Fung Pak-liu, joint founder of Li & Fung, preferred the modern method of recording transactions on paper. Something of a rarity in his day, he was fluent in English, having attended Queen's College—the Eton of Hong Kong—for a time.

Expanding steadily, the company's trade extended to bamboo and rattan ware as well as jade and ivory handicrafts. In 1937, when the Japanese bombing of Canton began, Fung Pak-liu's son Hon-chu established a branch of Li & Fung in Hong Kong, and there developed a good line in torches, exporting countless shipments to wartime blacked-out Britain. In fact the torches were in such demand that Li & Fung went into manufacturing themselves. Later the company became involved in exporting textiles and plastic flowers, cargo handling, and property—in fact its development mirrored the very peaks and troughs of Hong Kong's economic story. The Li part of the business dropped out along the way, and today the third generation of Fungs is taking the family business to the dizzy heights of a transnational concern, with a network of thirty offices in some twenty countries, all busily bringing buyers and sellers

One brand of firecrackers made by Li & Fung

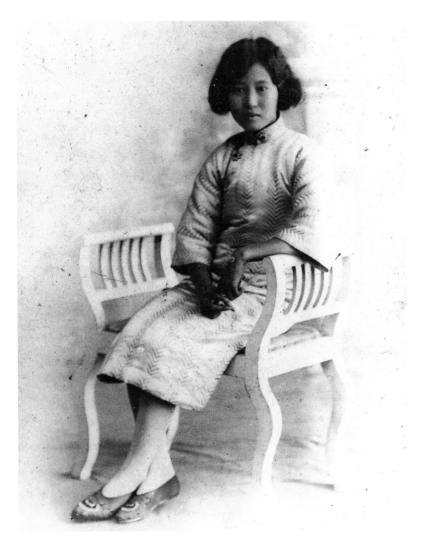

Portrait of a middle-class girl in 1920s Hong Kong

47

Sun Yat-sen

Besides attending Queen's College in Hong Kong, Sun Yat-sen was also a graduate of the Hong Kong College of Medicine. In 1895 he was instrumental in setting up a branch of the Association for the Regeneration of China in Hong Kong. In fact Hong Kong became a springboard for revolutionary activities, but the authorities soon removed the source of the trouble by banning Dr Sun from returning to the colony for five years. A similar organization, the Revolutionary Alliance (later to become the Nationalist Party) was founded in Tokyo in 1905; this association also established a base in Hong Kong. It finally realized its aim—to overthrow imperial rule—in 1911.

Sun Yat-sen was later to give credit to the British colony for enlightening him on how orderly government should be conducted. Speaking at the 1923 congregation of the University of Hong Kong, he said: 'Afterwards I saw the outside world, and I began to wonder how it was that foreigners, that Englishmen could do such things as they had done, for example with the barren rock of Hong Kong.'

Sun Yat-sen

together. Its chairman, Dr Victor Fung, and managing director, William Fung, exemplify the successful outcome of combining Chinese business aptitude with Western management techniques. Both are thoroughly bicultural and dazzlingly well qualified, holding, in the case of Victor, a degree from the Massachusetts Institute of Technology and a doctorate from Harvard, and, in the case of William, a degree from Princeton and an MBA from Harvard. 'The Fung brothers', *Newsweek* pronounced in late 1996 in an article entitled 'How to Succeed in Dad's Business? Go to Harvard', 'represent the future of Asian family businesses.'

But all this still lay ahead. In early twentieth-century Hong Kong, this growth of Chinese business created the need to establish Chinese banks—otherwise local businessmen had to conduct their banking through a comprador in one of the foreign banks, a service that came with extortionate rates of interest. A few years after the opening of the Bank of Canton, started by a group of Chinese returnees from San Francisco, the Bank of East Asia was launched in 1919.

The Bank of East Asia had nine founders of which two, the Li and the Kan families, were the driving force. As David K. P. Li, son of one of the founders, recalls, the bank was an instant success.

Strikes and Boycotts

In China, though a republic had been established, there was still a great deal more to be done to reanimate the country, and for the moment the Nationalist regime failed to muster the necessary strength. Rapidly fragmenting into regions controlled by warlords, China struggled to establish a stable government. In Canton, a revolutionary faction under Sun Yat-sen gained the upper hand for a time. Political changes on the Mainland as always cast their long shadow over Hong Kong. A surge of nationalistic feeling flowed over into the colony and that, combined with desperate poverty, fuelled a wave of resentment against the colonial administration. The average monthly wage of a manual worker in 1921 was around twenty-five dollars, somewhat below a family subsistence requirement of around thirty dollars.

Governor Sir Reginald Stubbs, who took office a year after May departed, was called upon to deal with the engineers' strike as soon as he arrived. Convinced that the labour tensions could be eased by cultivating good relations with Canton, Stubbs tried to play a mediating role by helping Sun Yat-sen. The Foreign Office did not approve of his initiative and said so; on the next occasion, the strike by seamen was handled with much more rigour and tougher action by the Hong Kong government. Relations between the colonial government and the authorities in Canton deteriorated rapidly, and by late 1925 an anti-British strike was in full swing.

The strike had been triggered in May when students were shot by policemen under British command in Shanghai's international settlement. Labour leaders in Canton immediately called for strikes throughout the Treaty Ports. Responding to the call, the Hong Kong unions demanded better working conditions and pay. In the space of one month Hong Kong was brought to a virtual standstill, the workforce having either downed tools or left the colony.

As the number of people on strike is said to have been as high as 250,000, a state of emergency had to be declared. Then another clash between demonstrators in Canton and British authorities, resulting in casualties, hardened attitudes and led to a trade boycott of the British colony. 'Hong Kong is the throat of China's economy . . . she has a stranglehold over us. Let us throttle her and open up a new outlet of our own in Canton,' announced the strike committee. This action completely disrupted shipping between Hong Kong and Canton and precipitated several bank runs in the colony.

Some sixteen million dollars were withdrawn from local banks within the space of three days. Governor Stubbs hastily ordered a ceiling on payment of not more than 10 per cent of all deposits, but by then the general loss of confidence was threatening to pull down the banks one after another. David Li tells how his grandfather, Li Koon-chun, ensured the survival of the Bank of East Asia by emptying his safe at home and putting his own gold bullion in the bank's window. Apparently this show of personal wealth was enough to convince customers that his bank was solid.

Stubbs left office before a resolution of the labour dispute was reached, and was replaced by Sir Cecil Clementi. It was quickly evident to Clementi that 'The sooner the present sore which is festering and may become chronic can be healed, the better it will be for British interests not only in Hong Kong but throughout China.' As it happened, the sore more or less healed itself, aided by changes in China which, as ever, had a decisive effect on Hong Kong. What had transpired was the death of Sun Yat-sen, a coup which put power into the hands of Chiang Kai-shek, and the Canton government's withdrawal of support for the boycott. By October 1926 it was all over.

An enlightened man, Clementi had studied classics at Oxford and later became fluent in both Mandarin and Cantonese. A favourite anecdote told by his grandson, David Clementi, relates to one occasion when Sir Cecil was at a meeting with a northern Chinese (who spoke the Peking dialect) and one from the south (who spoke Cantonese); the two Chinese could only communicate with each other through Sir Cecil. Sir Cecil's time as governor, David Clementi observed, was marked by a significant improvement in Anglo-Chinese friendships. In 1925 the newly arrived governor saw and deplored the racial discrimination and inequality revealed by the strikes. Those were the days when young expatriate recruits were forbidden by their employers to marry local girls, and a

The inter-war period saw the expansion of a rich and educated Chinese élite; this group photograph is from the family album of Tang Shiu-kin (front row, in Western suit). A businessman with interests in diverse enterprises, including Kowloon Motor Bus, Tang was also a well-known public figure and benefactor of numerous Hong Kong charities. He is shown here at the opening of a new wing of the Tung Wah Hospital

A young Tang Shiu-kin with the colonial and military establishment

At Government House, 1911. The two seated figures are Sun Yat-sen and Sir Claude Severn, Colonial Secretary. Cecil Clementi, who later became governor of Hong Kong, stands behind (far right)

Chinese would find it almost impossible to reach a senior position in a hong. To the horror of the European establishment Clementi disregarded such taboos and invited representatives of the Chinese community to dine at Government House. He even suggested demolishing the Hong Kong Club, that bastion of expatriate aloofness, and replacing it with one open to all races.

Sir Cecil Clementi, Governor, 1920–30:

'My acquaintance with Hong Kong and with things Chinese now extends over a quarter of a century and nothing has been a cause to me of more anxiety throughout that period than the fact that the Chinese and European communities of Hong Kong, although in daily contact with each other, nevertheless move in different worlds, neither having any real comprehension of the mode of life or ways of thought of the other. This is a most regrettable misunderstanding which retards the social, moral, intellectual, and even commercial and material progress of the colony.'

After 1926 Sir Cecil turned his attention to public works and social issues: to exterminate mosquitoes nullahs were filled; factory laws were reviewed as was the use of child labour; the local system of *mui-tsai* (a Cantonese term referring to young girls sold as household slaves) was more closely controlled, though this appalling abuse was not abolished until 1931; a new reservoir project was instigated and the building of Queen Mary Hospital begun. Land was reclaimed from Kowloon Bay on which Kai Tak aerodrome would be built. During Clementi's governorship Sir Paul Chater died aged eighty. In his place on the Executive Council Clementi appointed the first Chinese member, Sir Shouson Chow.

If Chinese political representation was still severely limited, in the business world prosperity for the local community was growing

Approaching Kai Tak airport from the sea

apace. A wealthy, educated, and fashionable Chinese élite was burgeoning and was very much to the fore on the social scene, particularly in 1932, when a lavish double wedding wove together the families of a couple of Bank of East Asia founders. A daughter of each of the Kan and Li banking families—Ivy Kan and Doris Li—married the twin sons of Fung Pingshan, also a Bank of East Asia director. As one of the brides, now Lady Fung, recalls, 'It was the grandest wedding of the century.' The bridal and trousseau outfits, in a mixture of Chinese and European styles, were the same for both brides, but their dowries differed in one detail. The furniture that accompanied Lady Fung to her married home was in carved blackwood, whereas Doris Li chose a set of sofas in European style. A reception for 1,500 guests was held on three floors of the Kan Chinese Emporium.

The banking families of Kan, Li, and Fung were joined in a double wedding in 1932

Fireworks and a lion dance marking the coronation of King George VI, 1937

Battle at Wong Nai Chung Gap, which resulted in heavy casualties of both British and Japanese troops. This is a painting by a Japanese war artist

War with Japan

In China, although Chiang Kai-shek and the Nationalist army had succeeded in gaining control over most of the country, the political situation remained chaotic and new problems loomed. The two main threats to a precariously maintained stability were military aggression from Japan and the rise of communism. In 1937 the Japanese bombing of Shanghai effectively marked the beginning of the Second World War for China. Suddenly 250,000 refugees were flooding into Hong Kong. Impossible demands were made on an already overcrowded city: some 30,000 were sleeping on the streets the following summer, forcing the colonial government to open temporary camps and commandeer railway wagons to accommodate the overflow. Civic order was maintained but only by means of stringent controls and censorship. This time the refugees brought with them not just a desperate need but, eventually, a new richness to Hong Kong's cultural life, for among the influx were writers, journalists, and artists. For an interlude Hong Kong was also helped by the diversion of Shanghai-bound cargoes to its own port as well as by the relocation to the colony of such strategic institutions as the Bank of China.

But this was to be only a temporary respite, for soon Hong Kong's back was against the wall too. In October 1938 Canton was taken by the advancing Japanese army. By the following year the border station of Lo Wu in the New Territories was being bombed. Hong Kong itself was a hotbed of Japanese spies and collaborators. The most infamous of these was the Hong Kong Hotel barber who

Ship fired on by Japanese bombers

had cut the hair of two governors and who, on the day of the Japanese occupation, presented himself to Governor Sir Mark Young, in the uniform of a commander of the Imperial Japanese Navy.

The colony prepared for the worst: when conscription was announced, the able-bodied joined the Hong Kong Volunteer Defence Corps, the Naval Defence Force, or the Volunteer Special Guard Company. Air raid shelters were hurriedly built; black-outs were put in place; the beaches and harbour were mined; and a tax was introduced, not only to fund the defence works, but also to remit money to China in support of the war effort. Some European women and children were evacuated to Australia. While many in Hong Kong viewed the prospect of a Japanese attack with a mixture of disbelief and complacency, the British government's private attitude was fatalistic; Churchill, justifying his decision not to send reinforcements, wrote: 'If Japan goes to war with us there is not the slightest chance of holding Hong Kong or relieving it.'

In one of the most vivid accounts of the Japanese occupation of Hong Kong, *Escape Through China*, the author David Bosanquet describes how it all began. Saturday, 6 December 1941, a 'beautifully fresh' morning: Bosanquet, a young Jardine executive, leaves for work. By six o'clock he is back home musing in 'a hot bath with the window wide open watching the shadows creep across Mount Kellet and a fiery sun sink into the sea.' He drives Joan, his date for the evening, in his old Ford V8 to drinks at the Gunner Officers' Mess. The brand-new governor, Sir Mark Young, and 'almost the

Expatriate staff of the Hongkong and Shanghai Bank under escort in Connaught Road during the Japanese occupation

Japanese soldier in a Swire refinery

53

East River Guerillas

During the Japanese occupation of Hong Kong the only armed resistance was mounted by the East River Guerillas. Originally formed in 1939 in Guangdong, this motley group comprised poor peasants, students, and seamen. Its commander was General Zeng Sheng.

Guangdong-born Zeng Sheng went to school in Hong Kong and Sydney. The resistance group he led actually obtained financial support from a Hong Kong body, the China Defence League. Led by Madam Song Qingling, the League members included people such as Hilda Selwyn-Clarke (wife of the director of Medical and Health Services), Israel Epstein (an assistant editor of the *South China Morning Post*), and Liao Chengzhi. Liao operated under the guise of an import–export firm called Yue Hua Company in Queen's Road Central where he solicited support and funds from Hong Kong and overseas Chinese.

Japanese soldiers taken prisoners after the surrender of Hong Kong to the Allies

When war reached Hong Kong in 1941, the guerilla force grew from an initial group of 200 to more than 6,000 soldiers. In the wake of British retreat from the New Territories, Zeng and his soldiers picked up the abandoned weapons and established bases there as well as in urban Kowloon. Adopting classic guerilla tactics, they killed a number of Chinese collaborators to cut off sources of intelligence to the Japanese. Protection was given to small-time traders plying between Kowloon and southern China. The guerillas also engaged in extensive sabotage activities, such as the bombing of the railway bridge in Kowloon's Argyle Street, the attack on the police station in Tai Po, and the bombing of Kai Tak airport.

whole of Hong Kong' are there, the men in mess kit or dinner jackets and the ladies in evening gowns. Dinner at Gripps, the fashionable restaurant at the Hong Kong Hotel, follows. As they finish dinner, Bosanquet receives an urgent message to return to the office. The news is bad: Jardine ships are to leave port without delay; the senior import manager has just arrived from Shanghai with all the important business documents in his briefcase and is to sail for India that night; he has orders to set up a Jardine office in India immediately.

Next day the tension mounts, though Bosanquet manages a round of golf at Fanling; afterwards he finds posted on the door of the clubhouse this notice: 'All volunteers mobilized. Report headquarters by 1030 hours'. At five o'clock the following morning, in another part of the city, Henry Ching, editor of the *South China Morning Post*, is woken by a call from Bill O'Neill of Reuters. 'Sorry to wake you, old chap' he apologizes, 'but I thought you'd like to know. The bloody balloon's gone up. The Japs have attacked Pearl Harbor and the Philippines. Britain and America have declared war. Hell of a show. They'll be here for breakfast.'

At 8 a.m. that same day Japanese bombers knocked out the few aircraft at Kai Tak aerodrome; later in the evening Japanese soldiers marched across the border near Lo Wu. They advanced down the New Territories in a three-pronged movement. With the defences at the Shing Mun redoubt destroyed—the Japanese threw grenades down the air shafts—a division of the 23rd Army was able to proceed quickly to the Kowloon peninsula. By 13 December Kowloon was evacuated; Lawrence Kadoorie blew up the Hok Yuen power station before boarding the last sampan to leave for the island.

Prior to attacking the island Lieutenant-General Takashi Sakai sent a note demanding a surrender to Governor Young. A Japanese soldier holding two European hostages brought the message across the harbour by sampan. The note ended: 'It [the surrender] will be honourable. If not, I, repressing my tears, am obliged to take action to overpower your forces.' Churchill would not consent to Hong

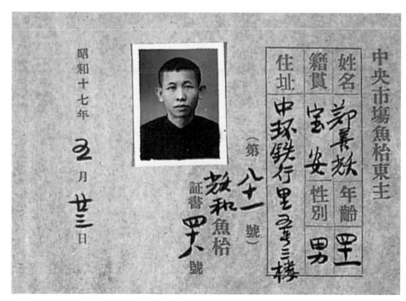

A licence to sell fish issued by the Japanese army in 1942

Kong's surrender so easily: 'The eyes of the world are upon you. We expect you to resist to the end. The honour of the Empire is in your hands.'

'The honour of the Empire' rested on a hopelessly ill-equipped defence force, brave but doomed. As positions fell the defenders were driven towards Stanley on the south of the island. The Volunteer Special Guard Company, which included many of the taipans, staunchly defended the North Point power station until their ammunition ran out. By Christmas Day the colony could hold out no longer. Despite the governor's last radio appeal—'Fight on . . . hold fast for King and Empire. God bless you all in this your finest hour'—further resistance would have been futile. On 25 December 1941 Young crossed the harbour to sign the surrender document in the Peninsula Hotel, which the Japanese had requisitioned as their headquarters.

Three miserable years of occupation followed. Under the governorship of Lieutenant-General Rensuke Isogai, Hong Kong became part of Japan's Greater East Asia Co-Prosperity Zone. Deprived of medicine, kept short of food (the relief supplies were often taken by the Japanese), and subjected to sporadic cruelty from their captors, the internees suffered. They were bundled off to Stanley, to limited accommodation offered by a fort, a jail, a school, and some living quarters. 'We had lived under the human bondage that the Japanese imposed on the people who were white, without hope of the days to

George Wright Nooth, former Assistant Commissioner of Police, describing Stanley Camp:

'Our basic ration was four ounces of rice for breakfast in the morning. The next meal was at about seven o'clock in the evening— another four ounces of rice and a teaspoonful of beans. Now and again the Japanese got a brainstorm and things like partridges would come. But that was only because the cold storage had been bombed by the Americans and they didn't know what to do with the partridges.'

Lieutenant-General Isogai

They rescued many prisoners of war, notably Sir Lindsay Ride, Sir Douglas Clague, Professor Gordon King, G. L. C. Pearce, and David Bosanquet. Intelligence filtered by the resistance movement into the prison camp at Sham Shui Po helped to keep up morale. It was widely known among the prisoners that if they managed to escape to the foothills of north Kowloon, they would be rescued by the guerillas. The East River Guerillas' most significant contribution to the Allied cause was their rescue of more than twenty US Airforce pilots who parachuted into Kowloon when their planes were shot down.

Officially, the main body of the guerilla group, some 2,400 of them, left Hong Kong for Shandong in north-east China on 30 June 1946. Some actually stayed behind while others provided constabulary duties in the New Territories at the request of the government for up to a year after the end of the war.

After the founding of the People's Republic of China, many of the East River Guerilla veterans rose to senior positions in the new regime. General Zeng Sheng was promoted to the rank of lieutenant-general in 1955 and became mayor of Canton and vice provincial governor of Guangdong. Chen Daming, who was political commissar of the group during the war, became vice director of the New China News Agency in Hong Kong in 1983.

General Zeng (whose wife was born in Hong Kong) actually played a significant role in the building of the water supply system to Hong Kong during its worst water shortage crisis between 1963 and 1965. His last active government position was as Minister of Transport. He retired in 1982 and visited Hong Kong in August 1984 to give his blessing to the building of the Anti-Japanese Memorial Garden in Sai Kung. General Zeng died in Canton in November 1995.

— Chan Sui-jeung

Japanese shelling of Hong Kong island followed the evacuation of Kowloon

come. We had received, for the most part, treatment such as medieval conquerors imposed on their captives, all the way from torture to semi-starvation,' Gwen Dew, an American journalist, recorded. The occupation, he went on to say, was 'one of the most tragic pages in the history of the British Empire.' But with the humiliation of the imperial representatives in the Far East, the image of the Empire had been distinctly tarnished, and was never regarded in the same shining light again.

Lawrence Kadoorie stayed in the Stanley camp a mere five months, and was then transferred, with his family, to Shanghai. 'They put two thousand people on a two-thousand-ton ship,' he recalled. 'It took nine days . . . and it was a pretty tough journey, particularly as my son [Michael] was only eight months old, and I was kept busy washing baby nappies in salt water. I don't know who it hurt more—the baby or myself. However, we survived that. We remained interned in Shanghai for the rest of the war.' David Bosanquet, incarcerated in a camp at Sham Shui Po, managed to escape. After weeks of preparation he and his three companions climbed into a manhole and down a drain, then by lying flat and pulling themselves along, they crawled out into a bay and to freedom. At the end of several gruelling days on the run they were picked up by some guerillas operating in the New Territories, given food and shelter in one of the Tang clan villages, and, thanks to the British Army Aid Group as well as the guerillas, spirited across the border into China. Eventually they made their way to the southwestern province of Yunnan, which had remained unoccupied by the Japanese.

Conditions outside the camp were not much better; in fact, the local population lived in terror. A pedestrian who did not bow low enough to a passing Japanese soldier would be beaten on the spot or locked up in jail. Many of the local Chinese fled across the border. Man-kam Lo, union lawyer and senior Chinese member of the Legislative Council, was put into solitary confinement until he agreed to sit on the Japanese Imperial Army Legislature. He resolved his dilemma by attending the meetings but refusing to speak.

When news reached the camps of the unconditional surrender of Japan to the Allies in August 1945, Franklin Gimson, the colonial secretary and most senior internee at Stanley (Sir Mark Young being

Australian correspondent with Japanese prisoners of war

57

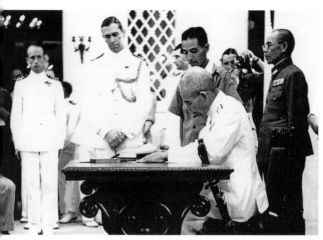

Vice-Admiral Fujita signing the surrender at Government House

The Japanese surrender, Government House; sitting at the table were (from left) General Pang (of the Chinese republican army), Admiral Harcourt, and Admiral Fraser

Arthur May, World War II veteran, with the Union Jack he buried during the Japanese occupation in a bag by his seat, at the Remembrance Day ceremony in 1996

Andrew Choa, member of the Eurasian community:

'I recall watching from the terrace of the apartment in Garden Terrace. A constant stream of people were going up and down the Peak. They were stripping all the boards and firewood they could find in the houses, and they were constantly being shot in front of our very eyes by the Japanese soldiers and left lying there. That was a daily occurrence.'

then imprisoned in China), immediately declared himself acting governor. Like Captain Elliot a century before, he took this step without any authority from London. Another inmate, Arthur May, had buried a Union Jack at the start of their internment. This was now unearthed and, to everyone's jubilation, hoisted. Gimson's pre-emptive action stunned the Allies, for, under pressure from the anti-colonial American government, Britain was considering handing Hong Kong over to Chiang Kai-shek. His action was ratified two weeks later when Admiral Sir Cecil Harcourt, to whom the Japanese surrendered, took charge of the interim administration and restored British rule.

Post-war Hong Kong was depopulated, deforested, and depleted of food. For Harcourt the priorities were 'freedom, food, law and

order, and a stable currency.' Sir Arthur Morse of the Hongkong and Shanghai Bank instantly honoured, at the cost of seven million pounds, the unbacked currency issued by the Japanese. A naval rating of the incoming fleet, Roland Davidson, found that food was a black market commodity, and 'could not be bought with money due to the fact that the Japanese had flooded the economy with forged bank notes . . . the ships had brought in a supply of new currency . . . it was a common sight to see rickshaws with suitcases crammed with worthless money and, later, owners emerging from banks with somewhat slim wallets of new notes in exchange.'

As he also noted, 'the organization that was put into force was fantastic. We had all our time cut out to stabilize the economy, to get the people back to work, and to restore law and order.' Hong Kong bounced back from its searing experience extraordinarily quickly. Almost as quickly, another blow was to descend. In 1949, post-war China and the world balance of power were fundamentally changed

A 1940s view of the harbour, with the Hongkong and Shanghai Bank rising above other buildings in Central district

59

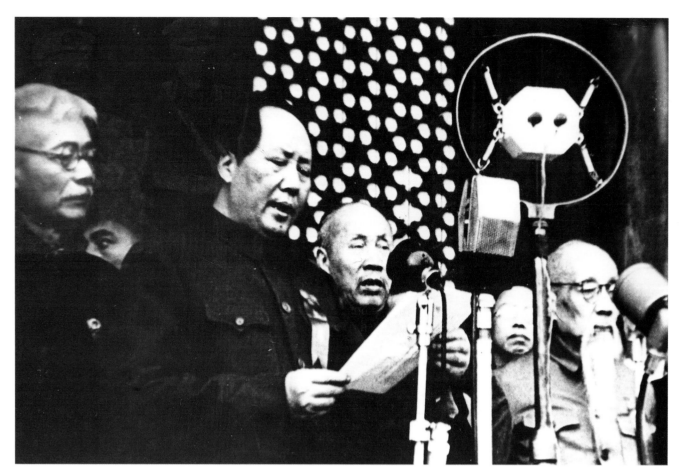

Chairman Mao declaring the founding of the People's Republic of China in 1949

by the triumph of communism. Of the many political events in China that have affected Hong Kong's history, undoubtedly Mao Zedong's take-over was the most significant. Its immediate impact, where Hong Kong was concerned, was to open the floodgates to huge numbers of asylum-seekers and refugees.

Han Suyin, the writer, described the Chinese refugees in Hong Kong in her book, A Many-Splendoured Thing *(1952):*

'We are all here, bankers, businessmen, rich women, missionaries and squatters. Those that take off half a hill to build themselves a home and those that crowd on a mat on the sidewalk to sleep. Wanderers against our will, we are the refugees. And to me, a transient among so many transients, that is Hongkong in April 1949: a refugee camp. Harbour of many ships, haven of people out from China, squatters' colony, fun fair, bazaar and boom town. Hongkong, where people come and go and know themselves more impermanent than anywhere else on earth. Beautiful island of many worlds in the arms of the sea. Hongkong.

And China just beyond the hills.'

60

CHAPTER 4

Workshop of the World

During the Japanese occupation Hong Kong's population had dwindled from about 1.6 million to less than 600,000. As post-war rehabilitation got under way, the population came flocking back at the rate of 100,000 a month. By the end of 1945, numbers had exceeded one million, this at a time when tens of thousands of totally destitute people still needed to be fed daily by government rice kitchens.

At the end of 1950 Hong Kong's population was 2.4 million. Had the newly established People's Republic of China not closed its border with Hong Kong in November 1949, more immigrants might have made it across. Even so, after another ten years, Hong Kong's population had risen to three million. These figures tell a stark story: what Hong Kong confronted in the two decades after the war was the near-impossible task of generating the means at a sufficiently fast pace to support its exploding refugee population.

Hong Kong had few resources apart from its deep natural harbour. As a result of the Korean War, the United Nations voted to impose an embargo on strategic goods to the People's Republic; the United States went further, with a blanket embargo on all trade with China. This policy penalized Hong Kong as well as the Mainland. The colony's entrepôt trade threatened to vanish overnight and Hong Kong, having always lived off its possession of the best harbour in southern China, suddenly had to live on its own. Britain, engaged in physical and economic reconstruction herself, was anxious to see her colony remain financially self-supporting, so no help could be looked for there.

In 1951, the American magazine *Pathfinder* was dismissive of the colony's chances of survival. Under the heading 'Red Market Place', it told its readers: 'Chiang Kai-shek's regime used to buy heavily of luxury goods like nylons and lipsticks in Hong Kong. Red

At the 1966 industrial fair

China scorns luxury items and buys only essentials. Its chief purchases in Hong Kong have been rubber and tires, iron and steel, cotton and textiles, penicillin and other drugs, gasoline, kerosene and oil. Some of this material goes to China by regular channels; some is smuggled in. . . . So long as Mao can buy Western goods in Hong Kong, the British Crown Colony appears safe from the threat of communist invasion. But if and when the UN imposes sanctions and Hong Kong merchants run out of supplies, it's a fair bet that Hong Kong may become a ghost city or a target from Red attack—or both.'

Thrown upon its own wits, embattled Hong Kong, under the post-war governor, Alexander Grantham, struggled to adapt to its drastically altered role. Fortunately the men and the means were at hand. Fleeing ahead of the People's Liberation Army were, among others, thousands of manufacturers and entrepreneurs determined not to lose everything to communism. These were not just refugees from Guangdong, Hong Kong's traditional source of immigrants, but also from centres further afield such as Shanghai, Wuxi, Suzhou, and Ningbo. Unlike previous generations of immigrants, these newcomers were not peasants nor the dispossessed poor. They had capital, equipment, and expertise. Cheap labour was already available, and more was arriving by the minute—immigrants continued to come throughout the next three decades, many of them illegally. What the wealthier new arrivals did was nothing less than setting Hong Kong on the road to industrialization and providing its people with a new livelihood. From these beginnings the phoenix rose out of the ashes and one of the world's greatest manufacturing workshops was born.

Overcrowding in 1950s Hong Kong meant much of life spilled out into the streets

Sour Sweet *by Timothy Mo is a novel about a Hong Kong Chinese family in England. Chen works in a Chinese restaurant in Soho, having emigrated from his New Territories village in the 1960s. He married his wife, Lily, in Hong Kong.*

'Lily was twenty-three then. To marry Chen she had to break the contract she had made three years ago with the Tsuen Wan wig factory which employed her as a stitcher. Its salient clause prohibited her from marrying for the next five years. With the rest of the female work-force Lily lived in a barracks on the factory roof, as she had done previously in crocodile shoe, ornamental cigarette lighter, gramophone, and transistor radio factories. The dormitory was one hundred and thirty feet long and fifteen wide, accommodating a hundred and twenty workers in sixty bunk beds. She had gone to the dance where she met her future husband with five other factory girls. This had entailed breaking the works curfew of 9 p.m. In case they were stopped by the police, who would have returned them to the barracks, they had all clipped a ten dollar note to their identity cards. The factory wages were fair and the girls did not resent paying the police their tea-money. Certainly Lily earned more than she would have done as a servant in either a foreign or a Chinese household where the hours worked effectively amounted to a curfew anyway.'

Hong Kong was one the world's largest suppliers of cheap plastic toys

What the workshops churned out was not anything grand or fancy. First and foremost it was cotton, since the most common industry brought by the immigrants was spinning; then it was consumer artefacts of the most basic kind. 'Made in Hong Kong' became a byword for cheap and tawdry or dubious goods—an image which had to be overcome later when low-cost manufacturing moved to Thailand, Indonesia, and China. The classic Hong Kong products of the 1950s and 1960s, besides textiles, were those catering to short-term crazes in Western markets: plastic flowers, wigs, clockwork toys, and the like.

Hong Kong's first plastics factory opened in 1947 just in time to catch the world plastics boom. A young man from Chaozhou (Chiuchow), his education truncated by his father's untimely death and working as a salesman of plastic belts and watch straps at the time, saw his opportunity. Before he was twenty-two years old, Li Ka-shing had launched his own plastics company, Cheung Kong. He also recovered fast enough from the international trade embargo to diversify into artificial flowers ahead of much of the competition. One of his best-selling lines was the hydrangea, and he would one day be called the King of Plastic Flowers. Still later, he would become the epitome of rags-to-riches success and the wealthiest tycoon of Hong Kong.

Textile factory

Those Arrogant Shanghainese

Textiles saved Hong Kong. Founded on cotton spinning, the textile industry expanded and gave Hong Kong an economic growth of some 10 per cent a year during the 1950s and 1960s. Raw cotton from the United States, Pakistan, and East Africa was turned into

63

Anna Sohmen, eldest daughter of Sir Y. K. Pao, in Hong Kong Remembers:

'The Shanghainese who arrived in Hong Kong in the late 1940s were very much a clique and kept themselves decidedly separate, mainly because we didn't speak the Cantonese dialect, but there were also cultural differences. We were really rather toffee-nosed. "We Shanghainese don't eat snake, and eating dog is barbaric. Those sorts of habits only belong to the Southerners". That's what we were told.'

Dyeing factory in north Kowloon

yarn in the dark satanic mills of north Kowloon. Gradually, as skills were learnt, the yarn was woven and made up into T-shirts and—most emblematic of Hong Kong's manufacturing in the mid-1970s—denim jeans. The garments were exported of course, in such large quantities that the overseas markets took fright and a quota system was imposed. Everyone thought that this was the end of Hong Kong's fledgling textile and garment industry, but it was exactly what was needed to push it to a higher level of technology, skills, and value. Entrepreneurs and workers rose to the challenge magnificently, demonstrating the flexibility and talent for improvisation which are so much a hallmark of Hong Kong's industrial sector. Since the quota system was based on quantity rather than value, T-shirts were abandoned in favour of silk fashions until, at last, the 'Made in Hong Kong' label was no longer anything to be ashamed of, but proudly displayed on the most famous designer names.

Gerry Forsgate, businessman and former chairman of the Urban Council:

'I was running the storage department of Kowloon Wharf and my clerk said there was a Shanghai gentleman who would like to see me. The gentleman was holding a bunch of godown warrants, the title deeds to goods in storage.

"I'd like to take delivery of it," he said in a hesitant sort of way. "It's been stored for nearly two years, and I intend to start a spinning factory."

I looked surprised and said, "There's no water, and there's no labour."

He said, "Water doesn't really matter for spinning. Labour—we'll bring it with us."

"What about the storage charges?" I reminded him. "Have you any money?"

The gentleman answered, "No, I haven't, but the bank will look after me."

And this is what happened. To the undying credit of the two major banks, the Chartered Bank and Hongkong Bank, they sustained these Shanghai textile industrialists, who eventually all set up spinning factories, starting at Tsuen Wan, until textiles became a tremendous industry and created something quite new for Hong Kong.'

The immigrants from Shanghai and its surrounding area who brought the cotton-spinning industry to Hong Kong were experienced industrialists. Many of them—entrepreneurs first and last—had been eyeing Hong Kong for some time. Japanese depredations and the civil war in China had disrupted business so much that the British colony had seemed a haven of order and stability. Commuting between Shanghai and the colony, they had been tempted to move, but Hong Kong's summer was so hot and humid—not at all conducive to cotton spinning—as one of them, C. C. Lee, discovered. Only when China fell to communism did they give up their homes in Shanghai. A journalist of the day found the lounges of the Gloucester, the Hong Kong, and other hotels 'crowded at "tea time" with refugee businessmen from Shanghai', while 'more and more of their old friends were turning up with each boat or plane arrival.' It was only when the border closed tightly shut that they finally cut their ties with the motherland.

There had been a Jimmy's Kitchen in Shanghai. The Hong Kong restaurant, on Theatre Lane in Central district, was a home from home for Shanghainese expatriates

John Shoemaker, American businessman and pilot, long-time resident of Hong Kong:

'We were evacuating plane load after plane load [from Chungking in western China to Hong Kong]. There were probably a hundred people wanting to get on the plane and we only had thirty-two seats. It was an old military style DC3. With every seat full, I got in and cranked up the engines and started to take off. At this time we could hear gun shot coming across the river, and this airport is right on the Yangtze river. As I was taxiing down the runway there was a whole family in a car blocking the runway, we couldn't get past. They wanted to get on the plane. Finally I had no alternative except to bring the whole family out. We put all their luggage and everything on board. Of course we were a little overcrowded but anyway we made it to Hong Kong. It was obvious Chungking was about to fall [to the communists], the agent had disappeared and we didn't get paid for the flight. I had my co-pilot pass around the hat to collect enough to pay for the gas. This last family had not paid for their seats so they paid sufficient to take care of the trip.'

C. C. Lee was the first of the Shanghainese textile industrialists to set up in Hong Kong, and today still keeps an eye on the business group he established. The group now spans the entire textile process from producing yarn to manufacturing clothes (buyers of which include Arrow and DKNY). Lee was the third generation of his Shanghai family to engage in spinning and weaving. In the classic mould, he set up on his own after cutting his teeth on the family business, starting the Dah Tung Cotton Mill in the late 1930s with 20,000 spindles and 500 looms.

Demand for textiles rose steeply at the end of the war with Japan. With characteristic foresight C. C. Lee placed orders for new spinning machinery from the United States. But getting an import licence from the Shanghai municipal government proved less easy. When the import licence failed to materialize he notified the

Spinning factory

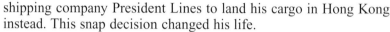

Garment factory

shipping company President Lines to land his cargo in Hong Kong instead. This snap decision changed his life.

C. C. Lee remembers those days well: 'I had to fly to Hong Kong to find somewhere to put the new machinery. Hong Kong had only small-scale cottage industries at that time. Sixty factory hands and managers from Shanghai came with me to supervise production and train up local workers. After a year I asked if they wanted to return to Shanghai, but most of them elected to stay.' Factory conditions were pretty awful. Air-conditioning was by no means prevalent, and in Hong Kong's climate only coarse yarn could be produced. 'Hong Kong produced only junk which we would sell at any price. Manufacturers took ten years to shift away from the cheap and nasty—I think that was the achievement of the Shanghainese. Of course we had no unions, but on the whole workers were not treated badly. Conditions were bad for everyone.'

Britain gave preferential terms to her colonies at that time, so large volumes of Hong Kong's textile exports went there. Locally, the government also provided incentives. Mr Lee's confidence in the British administration of Hong Kong was fully justified when it came to securing scarce foreign exchange. Rates were extremely volatile, with high premiums demanded in the unofficial market. The government came to the rescue by providing foreign exchange to C. C. Lee at the official rate. It was supportive too in smoothing land deals when he wanted to build new factories.

The Jardine taipan's wife, Lady Keswick (in tiara), greeting friends at a formal function

The Shanghainese had had a great deal of practice in manoeuvring their way through bureaucracy and commerce controlled by Westerners. For one thing many of them were English speakers, being graduates of American academies or such Westernized universities as St John's in Shanghai. In Shanghai they had counted Europeans and Americans among their friends: C. C. Lee's acquaintance with the Jardine taipan, John Keswick, was to lead to a merger of their dyeing businesses in Hong Kong years later. When required to speak to Hong Kong officials, they found English tripping off the tongue more smoothly than Cantonese. Not surprisingly, local sensibilities were offended by their apparent arrogance.

The Rong family was one of the most prominent textile families in Shanghai and provides another sort of case study. While most of the family dispersed after 1949, St John's University graduate Rong Desheng stayed, and was succeeded by his fourth son, Yiren, in the family textile firm. In due course Rong Yiren—and later *his* son

66

Rong Zhijian—would emerge as the urbane, entrepreneurial 'red capitalists' of post-Mao China.

Representing less than 5 per cent of the population in Hong Kong, the Shanghainese controlled some 80 per cent of the cotton-spinning industry. Textiles taipans were just one part of the picture though; there were others, possessed of the same entrepreneurial genius and energy, who came to Hong Kong in the late 1940s and early 1950s. Their finest hour would occur in the 1980s, but we find that they, too, made good use of their time in post-war Hong Kong. Several of them became household names in the colony.

Tung Chao-yung (more familiarly known as C. Y. Tung), born to parents from Ningbo, formed his first shipping company before the age of thirty. His Chinese Maritime Trust, both a trust company and a ships' agent handling British and Panamanian flagships plying the China coast, was actually registered in Hong Kong. Its operations, suspended by the Japanese occupation, could not be immediately resumed in 1945, so the company re-opened in Shanghai instead. Shrewd businessman that he was, C. Y. Tung decided on another move not long afterwards: he returned to Hong Kong, and opened an offshoot in Taiwan at the same time. Later, when goods began to be shipped in containers, the Tung liners were among the first to be converted to accommodate them, quickly introducing container services under a new rubric, OOCL (Orient Overseas Container Line).

When Hong Kong became the world's largest independent shipowning centre, it was hard to say which of the two resident shipping giants had the leading edge. The C. Y. Tung empire could boast eleven million tons at one time; its oil tankers, bulk carriers, containers, and passenger liners slid fast and furious down slipways in the great age of shipbuilding. Pao Yue-kong (Y. K. Pao) was the other 'Lord of the Sea'. For *his* shipping empire, the crest of the wave was probably in the late 1970s, when total tonnage reached some twenty million.

In fact, Y. K. Pao, another son of Ningbo, was first destined for the family business. However, the Paos' shoe and hat shop in Hankou, on the Yangtze River, failed to hold his interest for long. After some insurance and banking experience in the provinces, he

Tung family portrait, 1946. Chee-hwa (in front, second from right), the eldest son of C. Y. Tung and his wife, would later become Chief Executive of the Special Administrative Region of Hong Kong

Family group: Mr and Mrs Y. K. Pao and their four daughters (behind, from left to right) Doreen, Bessie, Anna, and Cissie

At low-tide this Shau Kei Wan slum became a stinking swamp

Celebrations for the coronation of Queen Elizabeth II, 1953

arrived on the Shanghai scene just after the Japanese surrender in 1945, and was promptly asked to take over the assets of the Yokohama Specie Bank and to help set up the Shanghai Municipal Bank. Soon this promising career had to be weighed against the uncertainties of a new China under communist rule. In March 1949, two months before Shanghai fell to the People's Liberation Army, Y. K. Pao and his family—two of his daughters, Anna and Bessie, had already been born—left for a new life in Hong Kong.

The Paos' first home was an apartment in Seymour Road, Mid-Levels—a positively luxurious bolt-hole compared to the tin-sheet and cardboard dwellings of the pavement squatters. Pao's father thought that his son might try his hand in property, but Y. K. had other ideas: 'Hong Kong was too small and lacked vitality. Life was very insecure, I couldn't speak Cantonese and didn't know anyone.' Insecurity bred a reluctance to invest in immovable assets, so Y. K. went into trading. No doubt he handled some of those essentials—tyres, iron, and chemicals—mentioned by that scaremongering *Pathfinder* article. When the 'regular channels' were sealed by the United States embargo, the commodities went through other countries, finding their way into China through Macau, for instance. It was a trying business, to say the least. One relationship established at that time was, however, to prove enormously fruitful. It was then that Y. K. Pao became a rather special customer of the Hongkong and Shanghai Bank, through his friendship with its chief manager, John Saunders.

Y. K. Pao bought his first ship in 1955. Ironically (as it became apparent years later), the man he first approached with his proposition was George Marden, head of a Far Eastern shipping group with extensive interests in Hong Kong. The deal did not go through, and it was from another British shipowner that he acquired a second-hand freighter, which he renamed *Golden Alpha*. It was said that he named his ships in alphabetical order (as he did his four daughters), but he must have run out of letters rather quickly as one freighter soon turned into forty, and a decade later the fleet included not just aged freighters but entirely new tankers and carriers.

68

If the oil crisis of the early 1970s irrevocably altered the economic balance of the world, for Y. K. Pao's shipping empire it signalled an equally momentous change. His strategy through the later years of this difficult decade—a reduction of his crude carriers and a gradual writing down of the value of his ships—allowed him to weather the shipping depression that brought many of his competitors to their knees in 1985.

Not all the Shanghainese émigrés stayed in Hong Kong; many of them passed through and went on to other shores. Diane Woo left Shanghai in 1949, grew up in Hong Kong, and is now a successful businesswoman in New York. Leaving Shanghai by boat as a little girl, she heard someone say, 'Turn round and take a look at Broadway Mansions, you will never see it again.' Her grandmother, on the other hand, had reassured her, 'Don't worry, you'll be back in Shanghai soon; just think of the Hong Kong trip as a holiday.' The holiday was to last thirty years. As soon as China's doors opened to foreign investors, Diane Woo, with her cross-cultural experiences, became a successful go-between for American businesses.

Many who could not enter Hong Kong legally found other means: in the bottom of fishing boats, through holes cut in barbed wire, even by swimming to remote beaches. To one such illegal immigrant, the initial impression of Hong Kong in the early 1960s was a blaze of light; to another, the first advertising hoardings he encountered—urging shoppers to buy seemingly everything one could ever desire—were utterly bewildering after years of socialist austerity.

Diane Woo (centre) with friends in Hong Kong, mid-1950s

Birds of Passage?

Here, then, was the world's largest sweatshop. The spindles and looms of north Kowloon, Tsuen Wan, and Kwun Tong whirred and clattered day and night. Factory hands worked twelve-hour shifts, seven days a week, in cramped and filthy workrooms, the damp air thick with flecks of cotton and the fetid odour of communal latrines. One worker—he was a mere teenager then—simply lay down at

People often entered Hong Kong illegally in fishing boats

Hari Harilela with his wife and Governor and Lady Grantham, 1957

night and slept on the packing table of the knitting factory which employed him. Later, as Jimmy Lai, he would become as well known as the Giordano chain of casual clothes shops he opened in Hong Kong and China. If the factories were grim, conditions for those who took home piece-work were no better. Finishing seams, sewing on zips, stringing together the petals of plastic roses, they beavered away under bare electric bulbs in squalid tenement buildings or tin shacks, a whole family to a room.

Many rags-to-riches stories had their beginnings in this period. One of them can be traced back not to a factory but to a shop—a shop selling silk goods on the corner of Hankow and Middle Roads in the bustling retail area of Tsim Sha Tsui. It was from there that the Indian Harilela family—father, mother, and children, including the second son Hari—diversified into custom tailoring. Hari Harilela knew what it was like to be made destitute, for the worldwide depression of 1929 had plunged the family into poverty and sent him and his brothers into the Kowloon streets, selling 'newspapers and whatever we could get'. World War II saw them floundering again. Hari's father, originally from Hyderabad, had been a successful trader of ivory and jade in Canton and Hong Kong, but he was ready to try a new business when his son suggested tailoring. Starting with a chain of shops making uniforms for the army and suits for a steadily expanding tourist trade, the Harilelas now have an interest in many commercial enterprises from restaurants and hotels to shops and property investment.

Hari Harilela interviewed for a Hong Kong radio programme:

'We went hawking to the British Army camp in Sham Shui Po. We would take a heavy suitcase and sit outside: we were not allowed in. We would sit by the gate and the soldiers would come. Eventually they felt sorry for us: it was hot and we had nothing to eat the whole day, you know.

In the beginning we suffered very heavily because my father always believed we should only have one price. [The soldiers] could not believe this because every hawker used to bargain. Once we established that we became very popular with those people. And gradually the officers heard about our reputation so told us to come to the officers' area to sell goods to them. Then we were given a very nice area outside the officers' mess. So we would sell to the soldiers in the morning and the officers in the afternoon. That's how we started'.

Of the several images typical of the 1950s and 1960s in Hong Kong, that of squatter huts on hillsides and pavements is perhaps the

70

Squatter settlement fire

most unforgettable. Certainly for more than 53,000 people, Christmas Day 1953 will long be remembered for the calamitous fire in a huge squatter area in Shek Kip Mei, Kowloon, which made them homeless. Not that squatter huts offered much in the way of accommodation; they were stuck on hillsides, one on top of another, and were no more than windowless tin-sheet or zinc-plate shells without plumbing or electricity. The widespread use of kerosene for lighting and cooking made the huts terrible fire risks, and open drains posed a hazard to health.

The Shek Kip Mei crisis did, however, force the government into providing public housing. Established the following year, the Resettlement Department began its massive programme by building, extremely quickly, estates of very basic six- or seven-storey H-shaped blocks. These blocks had no lifts and provided single-room flats, designed to give each adult resident less than two and a half square metres of space, and only communal washing facilities. At the beginning they were not even wired for electricity.

Napping at a bus terminus, Kowloon, 1956

Resettlement estates were an emergency measure which fell so short of demand that the shanty towns persisted in scarring many hillsides well into the 1970s. Similarly, the human invasion from mainland China continued to undermine the economic recovery of Hong Kong. Mao Zedong launched his hugely misjudged 'Great Leap Forward' in 1958. This was a campaign to accelerate national production, particularly of steel, energy, and coal. An enthusiastic but inexperienced populace responded to Mao's call but failed to meet his unrealistically ambitious targets. The havoc in industry that the Great Leap Forward caused was followed by a succession of disastrous

71

Lok Ma Chau in the New Territories, at the border with China

harvests, which pitched China into another maelstrom of chaos and famine. In 1962—since described as the 'year of the hungry tiger'—border guards on the Chinese side looked the other way as 70,000 starving refugees entered Hong Kong in the space of twenty-five days. Policemen posted at the Hong Kong side of the border did their utmost to stem the flow, but no sooner were many of the refugees caught and repatriated than they made another attempt to cross over. There were simply not enough policemen or fences to stop them.

George Wright Nooth, former Assistant Commissioner of Police:

'In the late 1950s they [refugees] arrived in their hundreds and thousands. They just came straight over the fence. The Chinese could have taken Hong Kong without having an army. All they had to do was just push ten million people over and keep on walking.'

Some of the refugees found accommodation of sorts, rented from landlords who exploited the scarcity, so that private housing was often more shoddy than government-built estates. Housing became one of the greatest anomalies of Hong Kong: first because, despite its non-interventionist social and economic policies, the government ended up housing half the population; and second because the estates often provided a better planned and controlled environment, at low rents, than any private accommodation except the very best.

No wonder Hong Kong became a city of gamblers, with mahjong, horse-racing and the casinos in Macau catering to all levels of society. Life itself, in a place with such an insecure back-

The movie queen Lin Dai, an icon of the age, who committed suicide in 1964

ground, was a gamble. Most people were too preoccupied with the struggle of living to have much of a vision of the future. Certainly the refugees, having witnessed the horrors of political campaigns, persecution, and forced labour, were not interested in becoming politically active. A feeling of transience hung about Hong Kong, and people's sense of being mere birds of passage was very real.

What political currents there were in this period tended to be centred on the rivalry between the Chinese Nationalist and Communist Party supporters who had moved into Hong Kong. This came to a head on the republican 'double tenth' anniversary of October 1956, when a dispute over some Nationalist flags hoisted on a resettlement estate led to a flurry of rioting. But though the pretext had been political, general dissatisfaction with poor living conditions was probably at the root of it all.

Queuing for water

Apart from the Nationalist and Communist Party supporters, most people in Hong Kong remained quietly apolitical. In a filmed interview Sir David Akers-Jones, who served in the Hong Kong civil service from 1960 to 1986, said: 'People forget when they say, "Why didn't you organize elections and democracy earlier?" I think it's well summed up in the words of Dick Wilson, who writes about China and Hong Kong, when he said to talk about democracy in Hong Kong at that time was really like trying to organize elections in a railway station.'

Relations with China were fairly harmonious during this period. This was just as well: in 1963, after a terrible drought, Hong Kong had to go begging for water, and Guangdong responded by piping some eight hundred million gallons a month across the border.

The early 1960s was a period of acute water shortage and rationing

73

Remembrance Day service at the cenotaph in Statue Square, 1968. The Hong Kong Club is on the left

Nevertheless the threat of water-rationing continued to be a fact of life. The standpipe surrounded by queues of people with empty water buckets is as familiar an image of this period as the squatter huts were of the 1950s.

Snapshots of the era also showed a great contrast in living standards. The wealthier citizens congregated in areas such as the Peak, Central district, and Repulse Bay on the south of the island, which were visually still very colonial, with barracks and cricket grounds, gracious colonnaded buildings like the Hong Kong Club and Repulse Bay Hotel, and detached houses ringed by lawns. People could be seen taking life at a much slower pace, and expatriate officials, even in the Secretariat, looked more casual than they do now, in white

Traffic policeman in Chater Road, Central district

Gerry Forsgate, businessman and former chairman of the Urban Council:

'During our early days . . . air-conditioning had not been thought of. We relied on overhead fans. People who lived on the Peak had to suffer water running down the walls during the months of March to June. The atmosphere was saturated with humidity at around 100 per cent. So we had a specially designed "hot room" heated by electric heaters, where we put all the bedclothes during the day. The clothes you put on in the morning were put in the hot room overnight. It was a different life altogether. The senior and junior executives of the Wharf Company wore white safari jackets and shorts with long socks. It was a very sensible rig. It was just the coming of air-conditioning . . . and all those merchant bankers that made everybody wear suits to the office.'

shorts, open-necked shirts, and knee-high socks. For some, life went on much as it had done before the war. An evocative portrait of the age is provided by a *New York Times* interview with two women in the mid-1960s, an expatriate and a Chinese. It is a charming period piece. The special correspondent gushingly reports that it takes Mrs Michael Herries, wife of Jardine's taipan of the day, twenty minutes to drive the narrow winding road to her home on the Peak, where the air is 'rarefied but not restricted'. Looking out of the sunshine-

flooded windows on to the tennis court of her residence, Mrs Herries admits that 'It's an enormously comfortable life.' Her comforts, continues the article, include four house servants, two gardeners, a driver for her navy blue Humber, and a weekend house with swimming pool in the Shek O district (on the southwest of the island) near the still exclusive Shek O Club. 'The blue and white drawing room houses art objects dating from Mr Herries's years at Eton and Cambridge,' the interviewer informs us. 'Entertaining is divided between informal luncheon buffets for twenty-five at the Jockey Club, larger parties in the fourteenth-floor penthouse at business headquarters, Jardine House, and smaller dinner parties at home.' Her time is shared among her children—'if one isn't careful, days can go by without seeing them'—charity work, entertaining, or being entertained. One of those children, Robert, returned to the Jardine fold as a merchant banker in the 1990s.

At a Jardine's gathering of women executives and wives

For Mrs Harold Lee, the other interviewee, eleven servants are necessary to run the family mansion, looted during the Japanese occupation and now being restored to its former glory. In 1965, the article explains, Mrs Lee is in the process of buying furniture, but, as both she and her husband 'insist on old and authentic pieces, the acquisitions have taken some time. They include an opium bed strewn with brocade pillows and two hand-carved blackwood sofas from Canton . . . a pair of 200-year-old carved Peking screens . . . a deep blue Chinese carpet, which sets off the gold Thai silk upholstery of the drawing room sofa and chairs. . . . The dining chandeliers, a pair of specially made Murano glass designs, are among the few objects not Chinese.' It all sounds very grand. The opium bed is an especially nice touch; the correspondent fails to mention that Mrs Lee's husband is the younger son of opium 'godfather' Lee Hysan.

The Revolution Overflows

Michael Herries made some shrewd investments for Jardine's in the late 1960s. One example was his purchase, as chairman of Hongkong Land, of a building in Tsim Sha Tsui named Star House at a bargain-basement price. His timing might have struck other people as odd, for the deal was done at the height of a period of political disturbances in Hong Kong. In April 1966 an outbreak of riots in Kowloon in protest against a tiny increase in the first-class fare for the Star Ferry cross-harbour service was the first sign of unrest, but much more violent and widespread disturbances were to ensue.

Mr and Mrs Michael Herries

Gerry Forsgate, businessman and former chairman of the Urban Council:

'There was a build-up of tension from the beginning of 1967. The ferry operators were very belligerent. At every staff meeting I attended, they brought their "little red books" and we brought ours, and we argued the toss.

It was not labour against management so much as political. They were really looking for all the major industrial and service companies like the ferries and Wharf to admit they were wrong. Posters kept being put up, and we kept taking them down. It was an absolutely bizarre situation.

Then I got news that there was the possibility of a strike. In fact the Star Ferry service stopped. It was about the third week in May. Then I heard that the chaps at Wharf were going to stop work as well, in sympathy. . . . But as soon as we stopped our service [the Yau Ma Tei ferry] there was a bunch of junks, motor boats, *walla wallas*, to carry people across the harbour. Where the ferry would charge a few cents, these would carry people for a few dollars, so I would say the entrepreneurship of the average Hong Kong guy was alive and well.'

A flying boat

This unhappy period of Hong Kong's story really began in Macau, the Portuguese possession across the Pearl River Delta forty kilometres from Hong Kong. In the 1950s Macau was one of the most tranquil colonies in the world. For a time expatriate administrative officers from the Hong Kong civil service were sent to live in the Bela Vista Hotel there to learn a pure Cantonese unadulterated by Hong Kong slang. In this sleepy colony there was one Hong Kong government junior stamping entry permits; there was a shady casino; and there had been the world's first ever hijack of a flying boat carrying gold in the late 1940s.

But in 1966 Macau also became the first (and probably last) colony to be offered up by its rulers and rejected. This was the year

Demonstration in China during the Cultural Revolution

that saw the start of China's Cultural Revolution, a mass movement started by Mao to radicalize the young—who became the notorious Red Guards—and rekindle the heat of revolutionary fervour. It unleashed extreme chaos and lasted about a decade; during its most violent phase much of China's heritage was destroyed, millions of people were persecuted and killed for being 'capitalist roaders', and various factions of the Red Guards virtually waged war on their victims and on each other.

The torch that ignited the revolutionary fuse in Macau was a trivial incident. When a minor building infringement by a communist-run school there was handled clumsily by the Portuguese authorities, supporters of Mao mobbed the Macau governor's house, and troops had to be brought in to quell them. Within weeks Macau, whose border with China was always more porous than Hong Kong's, was flooded with Red Guards.

Damage to the Hong Kong government amounted only to the insults and inconvenience suffered by its one junior representative in Macau (although the official's wife is said never to have recovered), but another development had more serious implications for the future of Hong Kong. This was the rumour (later confirmed) that Portugal had offered to give up its 400-year-old colony, and China had, most extraordinarily, declined the offer. China was not ready to take back Macau, the Portuguese ambassador was told to inform the governor. It was a development that set minds wondering: did China also wish Britain to continue administering Hong Kong and, if so, for how long?

Protests of a non-political nature sometimes broke out during the government's squatter-clearance operations. The clearance of a squatter settlement on Mount Butler, Hong Kong island, was, however, very orderly. The inhabitants, given a deadline to vacate their makeshift huts, started at daybreak. Helped by teachers and students from neighbourhood schools, as well as trade union members, they formed a human chain to move their possessions down the steep footpaths. A keen schoolboy did his homework unperturbed by the commotion.

Central district, with a cricket ground in front of the Supreme Court, 1963

Demonstration in front of Government House, 1967

With Macau in chaos Hong Kong felt insecure enough, but sporadic demonstrations and riots by local trade unionists and communist sympathizers or 'leftists', which increased from the beginning of 1967, soon began undermining confidence even more. There were moments in 1967 when many people were packing their bags. Governor Trench himself was away on summer leave and was too ill to return, and other expatriate civil servants were said to be taking extra leave to be out of it. Those, such as Jack Cater, who remained earned their spurs that summer by staying to ride out the fight.

Although the leftists in Hong Kong were Mao supporters who thought they could best contribute to the communist cause by overthrowing the British colonial administration, the Peking leadership was actually ambivalent about 'exporting the Cultural Revolution', as the Chinese premier Zhou Enlai put it. In China there were frequent power shifts between the different political factions, not to mention rivalry among various Red Guard bands. The confused situation gave rise to some very mixed messages being given to the leftists in Hong Kong. At the start of the summer, radio announcements from Peking were urging them to demonstrate aggressively against British imperialist oppression. Yet some demonstrations were fairly tame affairs. Government House itself was the scene of a bizarre confrontation between some young leftist demonstrators and the police. It was described by the *Times* correspondent David Bonavia as follows:

Star Ferry—a fare increase triggered riots in 1966

'*Hong Kong, May 18*
The worlds of Somerset Maugham and Mao Tse-tung met face to face in Hong Kong today. Both were baffled. Long before sundown the tumult and the shouting died, and on balance it was a draw with points in favour of Maugham.'

79

Posters of communist heroes being paraded through Hong Kong streets, 1967

The demonstrators, whipped up by communist propaganda, waved their 'little red books' of Mao's thoughts, stuck up posters denouncing British imperialism, and chanted slogans. But when five o'clock came they all went home.

A further touch of bathos was contributed by the only casualty—the governor's pet poodle which, according to Bonavia, 'went frantic with indignation and had to be removed from the scene.'

Hari Harilela, leader of the Indian community:

'It wasn't a revolution, more like a tidal wave, going through. Those Red Guards or people of a communist nature in Hong Kong had no intention of looting or killing people. They were just trying to disrupt Hong Kong's economy so the British would leave, but no one came from Peking and asked them to leave.

I stood firm and a lot of people left. They sold their houses for practically nothing. If anyone wanted to, the furniture could be bought too. I did it the other way round: I sold my properties in Canada and brought my money here.'

There were other moments of bathos that violent year, such as when the enervating propaganda blaring out of the Bank of China building was drowned by pop songs and 'Colonel Bogey' coming from the Government Information Service office opposite, bringing wan smiles from passersby. By mid-July the disturbances had

80

escalated into terrorism with a series of bomb attacks. Over the next few months some 8,000 suspected bombs planted in various urban locations had to be defused; hundreds actually exploded, more than fifty people lost their lives, and many more were injured. In August, apparently reacting to the arrest of three editors of leftist newspapers in Hong Kong, Red Guards burned down the British embassy in Peking.

As the summer wore on it became clear that the majority of Hong Kong's Chinese citizens had no sympathy for the agitators, and veiled messages were beginning to suggest that Peking did not either. Bombings interrupted normal life for the rest of 1967, but calm gradually returned by the year's end. Nevertheless, the heightened sense of insecurity did not really pass until the arrival of

Sir David Akers-Jones, former Deputy Governor and Chief Secretary:

'People forget what happened in the 1960s, but it was just one damn thing after another. We had immigration on a large scale, we had one of the worst typhoons in Hong Kong's history, we had cholera, we had water shortages, we had bank collapses, we had the 1966 riots, and we had the 1967 disturbances, and that saw us through the 1960s.'

Governor Maclehose with his lively new agenda. Confidence was reinforced by an unexpected realignment of world power which put the United States in the same camp as China. Towards the end of the 1960s China had begun exploring a new direction in foreign policy, ending her self-imposed isolation from the world community. The United States responded by backing China's admission to the Security Council of the United Nations. Maclehose's arrival and the resumption of diplomatic relations between China and the United States came in 1971 and made that year the turning point of Hong Kong's story from recovery to economic triumph.

At the western end of Queen's Road

81

CHAPTER 5

Tiger in Transformation

The 1970s and 1980s saw progress in Hong Kong to a degree the world may never have seen anywhere. Yet the period did not start with great promise. The Star Ferry riots had given ample evidence of deep discontent and social division, while the post-1968 attempt to create better communication through urban district officers had got off to a slow start. The loss to government coffers of HK$450 million through Britain's devaluation of sterling in 1967 had been profoundly painful. Many officers in the Hong Kong Police, both local and expatriate, were on a bankroll of corruption; serving in a force that had been dubbed 'Royal' for its heroic role in the riots, they felt no one could touch them. Governor Sir David Trench, thought to have shown weak leadership during the riots, still spent much of his time on the golf-course next door to Fanling Lodge, his weekend retreat in the New Territories. Scores of businessmen and professionals with avenues to the United States or Britain had left.

China, its economy broken, was isolated, stagnant, in turmoil at all levels. Mao Zedong was ageing and his likely successors were fighting for his mantle. There were still Mao sympathizers in Hong Kong, of course, but the most radical of them were languishing in Stanley prison for their part in the riots. 'Keyhole reporters'—a term coined by the well-known correspondent Richard Hughes—regarded Hong Kong more as a China-watching base than a posting in its own right. One of Hong Kong's main tourist attractions of the time was Lok Ma Chau, a hill-top near the border from which to look out over 'Red China'. Otherwise Hong Kong was mostly seen either as a copycat market of cheap cameras and watches, or, with its tawdry Wan Chai girlie-bars and Suzie Wongs, as a playground for the stream of Americans on 'R and R' (Rest and Recreation) from the Vietnam War.

Economically Hong Kong recovered from the troubles of the 1960s with its usual adroitness. Entering the 1970s fairly flushed

Bruce Lee, whose kung-fu films invariably featured a lone hero taking the law into his own hands in the fight against violent gangs and criminals, was idolized by Hong Kong fans in the 1970s

American serviceman after too much R and R

Vietnamese boat people began arriving in Hong Kong in the 1970s. Because Britain obliged Hong Kong, as first port of asylum, to accept them, tens of thousands of Vietnamese had to be housed in camps while they awaited permanent resettlement elsewhere

with funds, in part due to careful management by Financial Secretary John Cowperthwaite, the government was affluent enough to embark on a spending spree, notably on improvements to housing, education, and the environment. Economic growth continued unabated, so that by the end of the 1980s Hong Kong was incontrovertibly one of the four Asian 'tigers' or 'dragons'—the export-led economies which were miraculously catapulting themselves out of Third World poverty. Moreover, seen against its historical background, Hong Kong was not just a financial wonder but a social miracle too.

The architect of this transformation was Sir Murray Maclehose. A 'watershed' governor between the old colonial cadre and the Foreign Office sinologues of the 1980s, Maclehose had both colonial and diplomatic experience. He served more than ten years in Hong Kong, from 1971 to 1982. Public housing on a gigantic scale and to a new standard was Maclehose's most visible and socially transforming achievement, but there were many other less obvious areas that he reformed. His contribution to education was perhaps as great as housing. Only in 1972 did primary education become free and compulsory, and within six years Maclehose had moved on to include junior secondary education for all too. An initiative which benefited the environment and reflected his own taste—he loved getting away from it all at weekends by walking in the New Territories and on the island of Lantau—was the setting aside of 40 per cent of the territory for country parks, a higher percentage than in any other country. At a stroke he prevented Hong Kong from becoming an urban sprawl, and provided the breathing space increasingly popular with a new generation of citizens for hiking, camping, and barbecues. Since then the 100-kilometre Maclehose Trail has become the focus of an annual fund-raising walk for Oxfam and other charities.

Equally important, both at the time and later as the spectre of graft and bribery resurfaced in the approach to 1997, was the creation of the Independent Commission Against Corruption (ICAC) in 1974. By his own standards, Maclehose was a little slow in moving on this. Top colonial officials had not grasped the seriousness of corruption in the police force and other

Governor Maclehose

Sir David Akers-Jones, former Deputy Governor and Chief Secretary:

'One thing to remember is that because of the way we collect our water from the hills, 40 per cent of Hong Kong's land area is country park. Beautiful mountains, beautiful woods, streams, rocks; wonderful walking country—and it will always be like that, even if the population reaches ten million. You can drive twenty minutes from the centre of Kowloon and be as lonely as though you were in the Cairngorms.'

Village clearance and a New Town Development Programme altered the landscape of Kowloon and the New Territories in the 1970s. Young villagers emigrated, many to Britain, leaving the older residents behind, like this Hakka woman living in Sai Kung Country Park

inspectorates such as buildings and markets. Brave junior officers who spoke out were sometimes sacrificed. One story recounts the experience of two young policemen, determined to take a stand against corruption. They kept a record of the regular weekly $500 in brown envelopes given them against their will, and then carefully deposited them in a separate bank account for evidence. When ready to provide this evidence to the Foreign Office to expose their seniors, they were referred back to these very same corrupt officers for investigation. The denouement was inevitable: the senior officers made it impossible for them to stay on in the force, so they had no choice but to resign.

In a speech he made in 1977, Jack Cater, Commissioner of the ICAC, indicated the level of syndicated corruption that prevailed in Hong Kong in the mid-1970s:

'I conservatively estimate that syndicated corruption has been bringing in to the corrupt a billion dollars a year. One thousand million dollars. That is, three or four times the annual profits from the worldwide operations of the Hongkong and Shanghai Banking Corporation.'

Not all uniformed officers were involved, and it was comfortable for a while to maintain the illusion that syndicated corruption was confined to the lower ranks and not found among senior expatriate officers. It took the exposure of the corrupt chief superintendent, Peter Godber, and his escape from interrogation with the help of his police friends at Kai Tak airport, to jolt Maclehose into taking tough institutional action. He created the ICAC and appointed the quietly dedicated civil servant, Sir Jack Cater, as its head. What underpinned the ICAC's wide-ranging powers was the unprecedented

A Chinese refugee caught in Hong Kong

Peter Harris, an academic, speaking about corruption in a radio interview:

'Confucius said: "When the state is well governed it is shameful to be poor and lowly, but it is also shameful to be rich and prosperous when the state is ill governed."'

President Nixon being greeted by Premier Zhou Enlai in Peking

article in its Ordinance requiring any civil servant seen living above his salary to bear responsibility for proving that he had gained the money legally. With such disincentive to flaunt wealth—and in a parvenu society like Hong Kong flashy display often proved irresistible—one of the underlying motives for corruption was instantly removed.

The ICAC was supreme for four years; though its wings were somewhat clipped at the end of 1977 when Maclehose had to cave in to police demands to draw a line and stop retrospective prosecutions, a totally new tone had been set in Hong Kong.

This unprecedented robustness in government had not emerged in isolation. Havoc was still the rule in China at the dawning of the new decade, but two dramatic events were—in retrospect—straws in the wind of impending change. In 1971 Lin Biao, touted as Mao's chosen successor, died mysteriously in an air crash. Even more momentous was an extraordinary development in *realpolitik* that same year: despite the adherence to hardline communism, China was suddenly re-admitted into the community of nations as the vital counterweight to the power of the Soviet Union. It was also in 1971 that the United States lifted the trade sanctions against China. The following February President Nixon of the United States, with the help of what was called 'ping-pong diplomacy' (because the first overtures were made through table-tennis matches), went on his historic visit to China which culminated in one of the world's most surprising alliances ever. Britain keenly followed suit and was also suddenly friends with China by 1972, five years after its embassy in Peking had been burnt down by Mao-inspired mobs.

With minimum fanfare, the United States acknowledged that Taiwan was a part of China. Shortly afterwards, Britain allowed Huang Hua, China's representative on the Security Council of the United Nations, to declare Hong Kong not a colony at all, just an internal matter for China to settle 'in an appropriate way when conditions are ripe'.

Looking back, it appears that Hong Kong was to pay the price for the resumption of cordial relations between Britain and China. Locked into this vague understanding with China, Britain no longer had any reason to prepare Hong Kong for independence, even though the process of decolonization of the British empire was almost completed everywhere else. If Britain's role in Hong Kong was as a caretaker until Chinese rule was resumed, then any attempt to develop intermediate forms of self-government in the territory would be pointless. Another step in Britain's disengagement was the Immigration Act of 1971 which, by introducing a more stringent definition of British citizenship, deprived those born in Hong Kong of their automatic right to live in Britain itself. Against this background, and for the sake of political correctness, officials stopped describing Hong Kong as a colony and began referring to it as a 'territory'.

It was fortunate for Britain and for Governor Maclehose that there was little local political movement at the time to protest. Hong Kong was less dominated by lawyers and intellectuals than by businessmen who were generally against democratic development because of its likelihood to increase taxes and government interference. Throughout the 1970s and most of the 1980s, therefore, this conservative attitude continued to prevail against change.

Boom Time

In 1970 Michael Herries retired as taipan of Jardine's, to be succeeded by Shanghai-born Henry Keswick, then only thirty-one years old. 'Yes, I suppose I am rather young for this job—but it doesn't frighten me,' the *Sunday Post Herald* reported him as saying on 21 June that year. He could not have known then that rivals to the supremacy of Jardine's were coming of age among the Chinese business community.

It was certainly Chinese punters who played the stock market and pushed it to new heights in 1972—though it was to demonstrate a tendency to plunge just as suddenly. But the roller-coaster nature of Hong Kong's stock market was still underpinned by an economy so astonishingly dynamic that it was to increase eightfold from the 1960s to mid-1985.

This phenomenal economic growth received the greatest fillip from China's adoption of the so-called Open Door policy in 1978. Deng Xiaoping's package of reforms, which heralded a gradual opening of a rigidly planned economy to market forces and foreign investment, created what economists call a structural shift in Hong Kong: in image terms it was as though Hong Kong mutated from grotty factory into slick, electronically operated office block. More prosaically, it meant that Hong Kong switched from manufacturing to services and became a haven of bankers, brokers, and fund managers. In a subtle way Hong Kong resumed its former entrepôt role

The Island Eastern Corridor was built during the early 1980s and opened on 7 June 1985

Deng Xiaoping, the architect of China's Open Door policy, in the early 1980s during a visit to Shekou, a forerunner of the Special Economic Zones near Hong Kong

Cathedral for Banking

The Hongkong and Shanghai Banking Corporation is the most dominant banking presence in Hong Kong. Its head office building, designed by Sir Norman Foster and completed in 1986, put Hong Kong on the world architectural map. This is an extract from an essay by Charles Jencks, the American architectural historian and critic:

The *raison d'etre* of [the] colonial outpost [of Hong Kong] is to make money, and no financial institution there is more powerful, or pursues its calling with such devotion and success, as the previously named Hongkong and Shanghai Banking Corporation (now streamlined with the new building and the shorter appellation). It prints currency, and to show its strength includes a picture of the building on the back of every dollar. Previously it was housed in a 1935

Art Deco skyscraper, 'the best building in the world' that money could buy in those Depression years. And so in 1979 and 1980 when Foster won a limited competition to design the new structure, it had to become the new symbol of strength for the year 1997, when the British lease on part of its territory runs out. From this two things follow quite naturally: the client, led by the chairman Michael Sandberg, kept asking Foster for the 'best building' possible, implying that cost was of little concern, and it had to represent power, stability, and technical proficiency—the presumed image of the Bank for the next fifty years. Hence the expression of massive structural 'bones' (at one point conceived in red, the symbol of Chinese potency). Hence the exaggeration of technical elements and some gadgetry (finally realized in another color of power, battleship gray). Hence the incredible cost, now conservatively estimated at [US]$640 per square foot, of what was proclaimed quite openly as 'the most expensive building in the world'— a part of its symbolism.

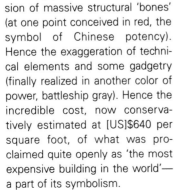

for China, only now it was not involved in fitting or careening ships, but in making deals. It became, in fact, China's broker to the world. Its integration with the economy of southern China also began at this time. Just over the border, the first Special Economic Zones set up in 1980 would take over from north Kowloon and the New Territories as Hong Kong's industrial hinterland, absorbing more and more of the manufacturing that Hong Kong itself could no longer support with rents and labour costs rising ever higher.

> *Sir David Akers-Jones, former Deputy Governor and Chief Secretary:*
>
> 'Over the course of the 1950s and until the mid-1960s the farmers in the New Territories gradually retreated from rice farming. Rather than spend weeks growing rice that wouldn't sell at a good price, it was easier to buy it from China and Thailand. So the New Territories began to change in the 1960s, and since then they have changed remarkably. . . .
>
> I think you've got to be realistic about the development of the New Territories. Although I am sad to see the paddy fields disappear and the old villages and their way of life disappear, on the other hand Hong Kong's population has increased from 500,000 in 1945 to 6.5 million in 1995. Our container port is now one of the busiest in the world, but it is not big enough, so we have to put up with storing containers on what were the paddy fields of the New Territories.'

Because of its location in the chain of time zones, Hong Kong seemed poised to become the 'third leg' (after New York and London) in the round-the-clock trading of financial markets worldwide. It offered other definite advantages too, such as the non-interventionist policy of its government, its British legal system, its superb telecommunications, and the use of English in business. This elevation did not quite happen, as the sheer volume of investment channelled through Tokyo made that city, rather than Hong Kong, the prime Asian exchange. But Hong Kong did succeed in weathering several financial scandals and crises in the 1980s and emerged as a stronger and better-regulated market for a sizeable portion of capital in the Pacific Rim.

With the arrival of the financial wheelers and dealers from America and Europe, a more cosmopolitan orientation crept into the local social scene. This internationalization took many forms, but was perhaps most glaringly apparent in the way the Chinese of Hong Kong took to foreign food. McDonald's swept the market, and those who previously would not dream of forswearing their lunch-time rice could be seen munching happily on burgers and sandwiches. Nightclubs became more sophisticated too, losing the sleaziness of those Wan Chai bars that catered mainly to United States servicemen. The yuppies that came in with the stockbroking houses and merchant banks brought with them a taste for the latest music, films, and entertainment; the 'chuppies' (Chinese urban professionals), as the local equivalent were called, followed suit. One particular nightspot developed dramatically in this period. Lan Kwai Fong, a seedy street just up the hill from Central district, had no attraction whatsoever until an enterprising Canadian, Allan Zeman, saw its potential. He opened the California Restaurant at about the same time as '1997' became the name of a bar diagonally across the road.

Pico Ayer makes some sharp observations about Hong Kong in the mid-1980s in his book Video Night in Kathmandu . . . and Other Reports from the Not-So-Far East:

'Where freedom meets money—that was the location of Hong Kong. And by 1985, the city had become the last wide-open settlement in the Wild East, the final El Dorado. This was where corporate cowboys came to lasso their futures, where fortune hunters flocked to pan for gold.

Change, of course, was nothing new here; it had always been the only constant in the hyperactive colony. Every seven minutes, the government erected a brand-new building, quite literally moving mountains and pushing back the sea and digging up new earth in its determination to keep up with the times. Nowadays, however, something else was changing, something deeper than the buildings. "In Hong Kong today," explained a Chinese banker from Harvard Business School, "to be rich is to be powerful. The two are the same."

Hong Kong was still officially the Crown Colony, but the crown was slipping off and the colony was slipping away. . . . In 1985, for the first time in history, there were more Americans in Hong Kong than Brits.'

One of a dying breed—the 'career' amahs, always dressed in black trousers and white tunics, who were still employed in many a middle-class household in the 1980s

It was not only the men who made deals. Women subscribed to the 'business and shopping' ethic in droves. Released from domestic duties and no longer constrained by lack of education or independent means, they bolstered the glamorization of Hong Kong. Joyce Ma, the doyenne of fashion retailers who introduced most of the French and Italian designers to Hong Kong, speaks of the women then as being 'very entrepreneurial'. She says that around the time when the Hong Kong Stock Exchange was formed by the unification of four independent stock exchanges in 1986, 'the ladies would come to my small shop as early as 8.30 in the morning as though on a treasure hunt, and new clothes would be bought before they had to be at their desks at 9.30. The "ladies who lunch" who didn't work would arrive from eleven o'clock onwards. In between trying on clothes they would telephone their stockbrokers, and I remember we had to put in four more telephone lines because the shop would be jam-packed with all these women spending a fortune on clothes and rapidly recouping the money from their dealings on the stock exchange. Sometimes it became so busy that our salesgirls and amahs were delivering clothes to offices, as those high-powered career women couldn't spare the time to come to the shop themselves.' Like the men, they offered stunning proof of the American economist Milton Friedman's famous dictum 'if you want to see capitalism at work, go to Hong Kong.'

Joyce Ma

Sir Y. K. Pao, after receiving his knighthood at Buckingham Palace, with Lady Pao

Another outcome of Deng's Open Door policy was an invitation to Sir Murray to visit Peking in March 1979. This seemed a timely opportunity to consult the Chinese government about the future of Hong Kong. With the imminent expiry of the term of the 1898 lease, land developers and bankers were worried about investing in the New Territories. But when the matter was broached, Deng was not prepared to be specific any more than Huang Hua had been at the United Nations in 1972. He merely said that Hong Kong's businessmen should 'put their hearts at ease'. Maclehose published this good news on his return; at the time he did not reveal what was said privately, which was that China expected Hong Kong to return to Chinese sovereignty at the end of the lease.

Investors were nevertheless reassured and business boomed steadily from this time. One of the most active investors was Y. K. Pao. He and several other Chinese, such as Li Ka-shing, were the new breed of tycoons, bolder and better connected than the likes of Sir Robert Hotung in his day. They took it upon themselves to initiate contacts at the highest levels—with the British as well as the Chinese leadership. Sir Y. K. Pao (for he had been knighted by Queen Elizabeth II) renewed contact with China as soon as the doors were opened to foreign investment, making an unpublicized visit to Peking and Shanghai in 1978. This was followed by an official visit during which he brought together Chinese, Hong Kong, and Japanese partners in a shipping and investment joint venture in China.

Pao was also the first Chinese to be invited to join the board of the Hongkong and Shanghai Bank. But he was not, however, the first Chinese to take over as taipan of one of the old established European hongs. This honour fell on the former King of Plastic Flowers, Li Ka-shing. Li's acquisition of Hutchison Whampoa in 1979 was—as he was later to claim himself—'a landmark achievement in the history of Hong Kong'. A symbolic moment, too, he might have added, marking a passing of the old order and an ushering in of a new period of growing self-confidence and assertiveness on the part of Hong Kong's leading Chinese businessmen.

On the verge of becoming the engine-room for China's modernization, Hong Kong needed new port facilities, office space, retail outlets, and residential property. The hongs were sitting on most of this capacity but their measured style was out of step with the sense of urgency and bustle of the local corporate predators.

Two other hongs changed hands in this period—the Hong Kong & Kowloon Wharf and Godown Company (known as the Wharf Company), and Wheelock Marden. The Wharf Company had been associated with Jardine's since the late nineteenth century. It was founded around the same time as Hongkong Land, and from the start it was the convention for the taipan of Jardine's to be chairman of the two companies. By the late 1970s, however, the Jardine shareholding had been considerably diluted. With a massive portfolio of under-developed waterfront properties and other assets, the company was ripe for the picking, and Li Ka-shing, the first to spot its undervalued charms, steadily accumulated a considerable shareholding. Wheelock Marden, also a British hong, had interests in shipping, property and the department store, Lane Crawford. As we have seen, George Marden had not been encouraging when Pao tried to buy a ship in 1955; thirty years later Pao owned 51 per cent of his company.

Hutchison, founded in 1828, had expanded too fast in the early 1970s, obliging its banker (none other than the Hongkong and Shanghai Bank) to come to the rescue by buying a stake in the company. Two years later Hutchison merged with its own subsidiary, the Hong Kong & Whampoa Dock Company (formed in 1863, as mentioned in Chapter 2). By then the Hongkong and Shanghai Bank was looking around for someone to take over its stake in the renamed Hutchison Whampoa.

The take-over battles furnished the business community with terrific excitement and have left their own corporate lore. The story goes that Li Ka-shing and Y. K. Pao had everything sewn up during an informal conversation in 1978. Apparently it was then agreed that Pao would facilitate the sale of Hutchison Whampoa shares to Li by the Hongkong and Shanghai Bank, if Li would sell his 10 per cent stake in Wharf to Pao. It could not have been as simple as that, but it did seem as if Li had acquired Hutchison Whampoa simply by asking the Hongkong and Shanghai Bank to give it to him, and that he had bought it very cheaply. Shortly afterwards, Pao made a bid for Wharf. After a flurry of secret meetings, dashes across the world by jet, midnight conferences, and heavy buying and selling, millions of shares changed hands, and Pao emerged as the new owner.

An assault was made on the Princely Hong itself. One day in November 1980 David Newbigging, the Jardine taipan of the day, left for London to lead a Hong Kong General Chamber of Commerce mission. One of the mission delegates was Li Ka-shing. On the previous Friday it had become clear that some extremely big players (including Li Ka-shing, it was assumed) were amassing Jardine and Hongkong Land shares, and that (in Newbigging's words) Jardine's 'was going to have to do something adventurous'. The decision reached by Henry Keswick and Newbigging in London was to buy enough Hongkong Land shares to fend off the raiders—a plan which could involve the expenditure of £100 million. As the weekend approached, and while articles for the Sunday papers in both London and Hong Kong were being drafted—confidently predicting the end of Jardine's—the firm was in contact with the heads of some of the world's leading banks and successfully obtaining commitments to fund its buying operation. On the Sunday papers, a campaign headquarters was set up in London's Berkeley Hotel, where the General Chamber of Commerce delegates were staying, and two direct telephone lines to Hong Kong were installed. A few hours later, while the other delegates, including Li Ka-shing, slept peacefully, the Hong Kong Stock Exchange opened to intensive buying by the Jardine team. By the time the delegates woke up, Jardine's had saved itself. Many analysts, aware of Jardine's dismal cash-flow, doubted the hong's ability to meet the settlement deadline; they were wrong, but the aftermath included several years of virtuoso financial engineering to stabilize the Jardine group's finances. When the mission delegates gathered in the Berkeley on Monday morning Li Ka-shing entered the room, walked straight over to Newbigging, and in silence shook his hand.

It was a short-lived victory for Jardine's. Before long there was another close shave when its huge debt, coupled with a property slump and an expensive attempt at diversifying out of Hong Kong, threatened to pull down the hong again. It had to sell off lucrative shareholdings in two utilities companies to ensure its survival.

Li Ka-shing

The Jardine building in Central

Peking meeting, 1984 (from left): Sir Geoffrey Howe, British Foreign Secretary; Margaret Thatcher; and China's premier Zhao Ziyang

The Joint Declaration

Even during the most heady moments in this period of hostile bids, soaring rents, and escalating share prices, some investors were nervous. In 1982, with the termination of the New Territories lease only fifteen years away, this nervousness took hold and the mood changed.

At this point the British prime minister, Margaret Thatcher, had just scored a victory in a much less significant colony on the other side of the globe, the Falkland Islands. She felt more than equal to the task of engaging with Chinese leaders on the question of Hong Kong. Sir Edward Youde had just been appointed to the governorship of Hong Kong. A diplomat with fluent Mandarin and long experience of serving in China, Youde seemed the perfect choice as a comrade-in-arms. He also rather hoped to write the definitive history of Peking, according to Lady Youde, but could never spare the time. Yet Thatcher's visit to Peking in September 1982 to begin talks turned out to be a failure. She had tried to set out a firm negotiating position by insisting on the legal basis of the British claim over Hong Kong and the validity of existing treaties. Unfortunately this stance alienated the Chinese leaders and deeply embarrassed the very people—the six million inhabitants of Hong Kong—whom she thought she was gallantly representing. When she slipped and fell to her knees on the steps of Peking's Great Hall of the People, in full view of the world's

Governor Youde

Negotiations over the Joint Declaration, 1984

David Bonavia (1940–88) was Peking correspondent of the Far Eastern Economic Review *and* The Times *of London in the 1980s. Living in Hong Kong at the time, he published a short book,* Hong Kong 1997, *the year after Sino-British negotiations began on the future of Hong Kong. He was at Margaret Thatcher's press conference in Hong Kong following her visit to Peking in September 1982.*

'Other comments of Thatcher's which were certain to annoy the Chinese—though they were unexceptionable in British eyes—were to the effect that Britain had a responsibility to the people of Hong Kong and that she shared the justified pride in what has been achieved in Hong Kong under British administration.

Mrs Thatcher left the next day, somewhat like one of those typhoons which roar in from the Western Pacific, leaving a trail of destruction behind them. Seldom in British colonial history was so much damage done to the interests of so many people in such a short space of time by a single person.'

television cameras, many in Hong Kong found it, in some obscure way, fitting. Thatcher then went blithely on to Shanghai, where she launched a ship for Y. K. Pao, later arriving in Hong Kong to a press conference at which, in reference to the nineteenth-century treaties, she offered her less than diplomatic opinion on China's trustworthiness: 'If a country will not stand by one treaty, it will not stand by another.' Local and international loss of confidence in Hong Kong followed swiftly on China's fierce reaction, causing a series of dips on the stock exchange and in the property market. Once more local people registered their nervousness by applying for immigration visas.

For a year the British insisted that the Chinese government would have to concede something concrete in order to get back the whole of Hong Kong, but local political support

After the signing of the Sino-British Joint Declaration, 1984

seeped away with the economic downturn and the uncertainties over China's intentions. When in September 1983 there was a steep fall in the Hong Kong currency—only saved by an ingenious pegging of the Hong Kong to the US dollar—the British had to think again. By then Thatcher had moved her attention to the wider issue of the successful struggle with communism in Europe, and had allowed her diplomats to take over the negotiations with China. She re-surfaced briefly on 19 December 1984 to put her signature to the Sino-British Joint Declaration on Hong Kong. This spelt out Hong Kong's future after Chinese resumption of sovereignty on 1 July 1997 over not just the New Territories but all of Hong Kong. The Declaration stated that the territory was to become a Special Administrative Region (SAR) of China, with a high degree of autonomy, and would maintain its freedoms and way of life, including its capitalist system, for fifty years from that date. The SAR would have separate executive, legislative, and judicial powers, as well as its own legislature composed of Hong Kong residents. It would levy and retain its own taxes. All these resolutions would be enshrined in a Basic Law, which was to be Hong Kong's post-1997 constitution. Deng Xiaoping encapsulated these unconventional arrangements in the concept 'one country–two systems' (*yi guo liang zhi*).

Hong Kong delegates attending the Joint Declaration signing ceremony in Peking in 1984

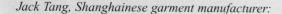

Jack Tang, Shanghainese garment manufacturer:

'After 1997 would China and Hong Kong be formally one? In fact, it is already one as far as industry is concerned. After all, Hong Kong invests in Guangdong industry where we employ five million workers, industrial workers—that's direct!'

Following what was perceived to be a successful resolution of the Hong Kong question, Queen Elizabeth II made a state visit to China in 1986

Deng Xiaoping and Rong Yiren, head of China's foreign investment corportation, in 1988

After all the previous uncertainty and lowering of expectations, the Joint Declaration quite successfully won acceptance in Hong Kong and was endorsed by the British Parliament in 1985. This was not the end of the story, however, but the beginning of twelve years of increasingly bitter diplomatic struggle. The detailed work of interpreting the terms of the Joint Declaration necessitated countless meetings in Hong Kong, London, and Peking. A body of Chinese and British diplomats, the Joint Liaison Group, was formed to tackle practical arrangements in the transitional period. It is widely believed that the stresses of those earlier marathon negotiating sessions contributed to Sir Edward Youde's death from heart failure during a visit to Peking in December 1986.

During the course of the negotiations, and when it was almost too late to introduce any significant changes to the territory's political structure, there was much rhetoric in London and Hong Kong about

Deng Xiaoping made this statement in the presence of Margaret Thatcher in Peking on 19 December 1984, the day the Joint Declaration was signed:

'The question that faced China was: by what means could the future of Hong Kong, as well as Taiwan, be resolved? There were only two solutions: a peaceful one and a non-peaceful one. To resolve the question of Hong Kong by peaceful means, we had to consider first the actual situation of Hong Kong, China, and Great Britain. That is to say, we needed to find a settlement that would be acceptable to all three parties. A socialist settlement would not be unanimously acceptable, and if it was accepted grudgingly, the result would only be confusion. Even if a forced settlement didn't result in military confrontation, there would be adverse consequences and a strong likelihood that Hong Kong would decline— and that is certainly not what we wanted for Hong Kong. Therefore, on the question of Hong Kong, the resolution that all three parties would accept was "one country–two systems", which would allow Hong Kong to retain its capitalism, its status as a free port, and its position as a financial centre. There was no other possible solution.

This concept strikes many people as new and unprecedented. To those who doubt whether it will work, we can only say that we have to wait for the outcome. But we believe that the concept will work . . . and our belief will be clearly vindicated in the next thirteen years, the next fifty years. We wish to say not only to our British friends present but also to the world: China keeps her promises.

A Japanese friend asked me, "Why fifty years? Is the figure arbitrary?" I said no, the period was arrived at after considering China's own situation. China has an ambitious objective, which is to increase her productivity enough to enable her people to become comfortably off by the end of the century. Even then, China will not be rich, but to reach a standard of living approaching that of developed countries will take between thirty to fifty years, provided that the Open Door policy is adhered to. . . . Maintaining Hong Kong's prosperity and stability is vitally important to China's own interests. . . . Fifty years was not casually or impetuously fixed on; it was defined in the light of China's developmental needs.'

Completed in 1985, Exchange Square (centre)
became the home of the Hong Kong Stock Exchange

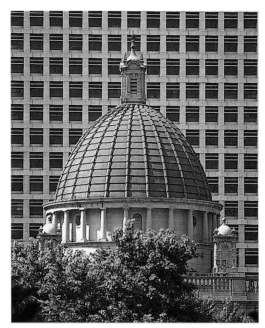

The Legislative Council Building

Basic Law negotiating session, 1985; David Wilson, who became governor of Hong Kong in 1987, is seated third from left

the possibility of developing democracy in advance of 1997. The Chinese government had conceded that the Legislative Council of Hong Kong would be fully elected in due course, but had not committed itself to a timetable. In 1984, after the wording of the Joint Declaration had been agreed, nods were made in the direction of progressively developing representative government in Hong Kong, first by the publication of a Hong Kong government Green Paper, then a White. The White Paper proposed a modest change to the Legislative Council through the creation of twenty-four indirectly elected seats. Building on this, it advocated 'a very small number' of directly elected members by 1988.

Peking, claiming that constitutional changes of such magnitude were contrary to the Joint Declaration, was outraged by the proposal. Feverish activity behind the scenes by Governor Youde and by his successor, another China specialist David Wilson, produced a form of compromise which satisfied China but slowed down the development of democracy in Hong Kong. In 1987, another Green Paper on proposed electoral reforms was put to the people of Hong Kong. Its contents were so convoluted and obfuscatory that most members of the public found them incomprehensible. A large enough response was nevertheless received to show broadly based support for direct elections to be held in the following year. It has since been reported that the government survey office which collated the public submissions shamelessly distorted them to suggest the reverse.

Once again, Britain and Hong Kong had retreated in the face of China's wrath. Without its own elected government, Hong Kong was now entirely at the mercy of those appointed by Peking to draft the Basic Law. The first draft of this document, published in 1988, elicited a lukewarm reaction from the public in Hong Kong. Political analysts and legal experts pointed out that though its guarantees sounded very fine, there were two fundamental problems. First, the Basic Law was inconsistent with the Chinese constitution, which defined China as a socialist state; and second, as it would be enacted into Chinese law, its clauses were subject to interpretation and amendment by the standing committee of China's National People's Congress. Hong Kong's high degree of autonomy, therefore, extended only as far as allowed by the Communist Party of China, which controlled the standing committee.

When the second draft of the Basic Law was published in February 1989, it was regarded in Hong Kong as an improvement on the first but not greeted with much interest. However, no sooner had the new draft been grudgingly accepted than the next political convulsion from China hit Hong Kong.

CHAPTER 6

'Same Bed, Different Dreams'

One hot steamy night in June 1989, the leadership of the People's Republic of China set the army on peacefully protesting students in Peking's Tiananmen Square. The violence of this act revealed an alarming aspect of a regime that had so recently been showing the world an essentially benign and reformist face.

Deng Xiaoping's economic reform programme, launched in 1978, had vastly improved living standards in China but had also created a whole crop of problems such as corruption, inflation, and wide disparities in income. China's leaders had long been split over the viability of a socialist market system, with the liberal faction advocating a faster pace of economic reform and the conservatives clinging to the principles of central planning. By the autumn of 1988, when the economy was overheating, and inflation had become unacceptably high, Deng's supporters had no alternative but to bow to the conservatives' insistence on retrenchment. This tightening of control went beyond the purely economic sphere. Liberalization had also nurtured aspirations among the population, especially the urban young, for greater individual freedom. To the conservatives, who saw all this as a dangerous threat to their authority, a crackdown on dissent seemed equally imperative.

Tensions came to a head in the following spring. Alienated students, more than ready to express their frustration and disillusionment, found their voice in paying tribute to a champion of reform, the disgraced Communist Party chief Hu Yaobang, who died on 15 April 1989. His demise touched off the demonstrations and calls for democracy that resonated in Tiananmen Square until silenced by the guns of the People's Liberation Army less than two months later on 4 June.

Rally in Tiananmen Square, May 1989

97

Support march in Hong Kong for the
Tiananmen protests, 1989

Li Peng, China's Premier, shaking hands with Wang
Dan, representative of the student hunger strikers,
Peking, 1989

What happened that night traumatized Hong Kong and released an outpouring of emotion on a scale and with an intensity never seen before. Earlier that summer, Hong Kong had shown its solidarity with the Peking protestors in various ways. On two consecutive weekends before the crackdown, an estimated one million people in the territory took part in spontaneous and disciplined demonstrations in support of mainland students. Gifts of tents and food for the students camped out in Tiananmen Square, as well as donations of cash and fax machines, flowed across the border from Hong Kong. A fund-raising concert was also held at the Happy Valley racecourse.

On 4 June the excitement turned to disbelief, horror, and compassion as the images of tanks rolling into Tiananmen Square were shown to millions on television screens around the world. These first reactions were quickly followed by fear and the recognition that a similar fate could well lie in wait for Hong Kong itself. The next afternoon people of all races joined a solemn march through Hong Kong streets. Hastily made black armbands were handed out to the marchers, many of whom had responded to the call to dress in black and white, the colours of mourning. Taxi drivers sounded their horns in sympathy and put up stickers in the rear windows of their cabs with such denunciations as 'Down with Li Peng' and 'Give us back our martyred compatriots'.

A day of mourning was declared the following week. All offices were closed as people gathered in Central district to pay their respects at the Cenotaph, the monument to those who gave their

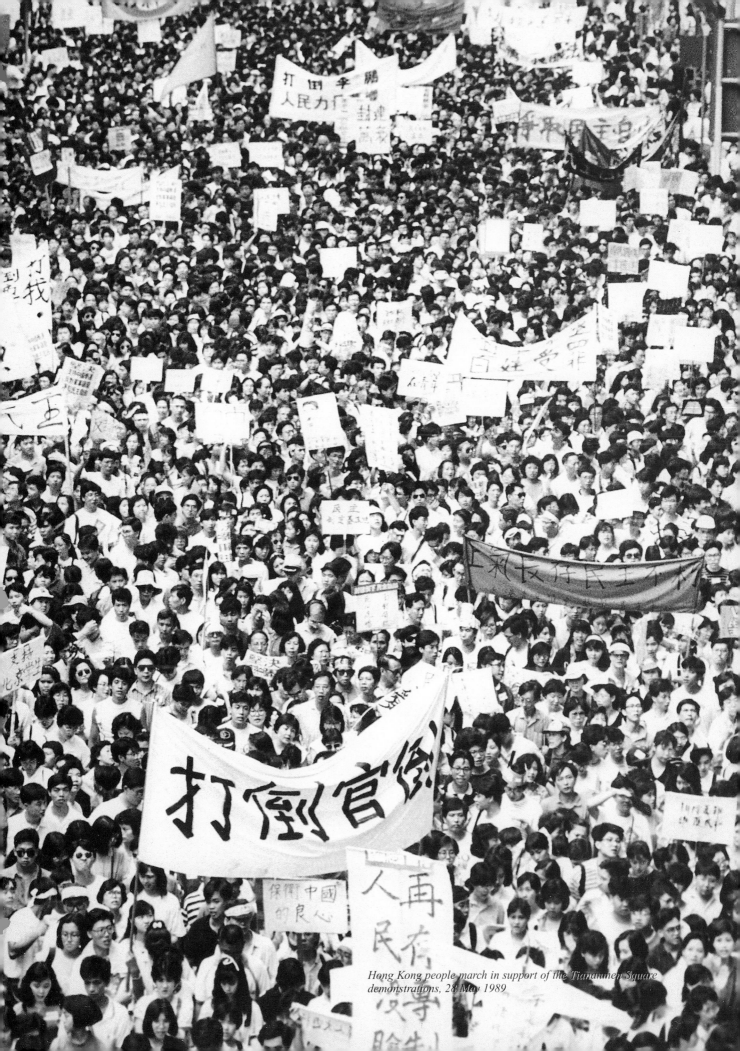

Hong Kong people march in support of the Tiananmen Square demonstrations, 28 May 1989

The Bank of China in Central district

Xu Jiatun, Director of the New China News Agency in 1989, spoke out against the Tiananmen repression. He now lives in the United States

lives in the two world wars. It was a sunny day, and distinct against the clear blue sky was the graceful tower of the Bank of China building, its gleaming facade gashed by a long black banner, hanging from its topmost floor, with an anguished message in bold white characters: 'Blood for Blood—Long Live Democracy'. Having paid their respects at the Cenotaph, the crowd moved on. A sombre procession snaked along Chater Road to Happy Valley and on to the headquarters of China's *de facto* embassy, the New China News Agency, where a formal protest bearing the signatures of all the marchers was to be tendered. Here the procession curled around the surrounding buildings, gently edging forward to allow the marchers to put their names to a scroll.

Within days of the crackdown some of the leading dissidents in Peking were spirited across the border into Hong Kong. Under the umbrella of the so-called 'Yellow Bird' operation, the dissidents would stay in Hong Kong for a few days before being found permanent refuge elsewhere. Such support to 'counter-revolutionaries', as the dissidents were labelled by China's leaders, provoked retaliatory action. When Yang Yang, an Olympic swimmer, escaped into asylum via Hong Kong in October 1989, the Chinese authorities closed the border against the routine return of illegal immigrants. This had always been an underlying threat equal only to the turning off of the water supply, half of which came into Hong Kong from China. A human flood would be as disastrous for Hong Kong as a physical drought, and only desperate diplomacy on the part of the Hong Kong authorities opened the door again. The economic repercussions in Hong Kong—as well as in China—were also dramatic. Trade and tourism suffered a severe decline following boycotts imposed by consumers and governments in the West.

Crisis of Confidence

Though trade recovered relatively quickly, confidence in the future of Hong Kong had slumped. Since 1984 Hong Kong's population had settled down to a quiet if unenthusiastic acceptance of the Joint Declaration and the draft Basic Law. Most people expressed little interest in politics except where their direct concerns were affected; their attitude was that basically the government should deal with the housekeeping and let them focus on the more pressing matter of making money. Peking's violent actions awakened them to the realities of political power and the critical impact it could have on their own lives too. Li Ka-shing, the taipan of Hutchison Whampoa, told the press in the second week of June 1989, 'I do not agree with the way the Chinese government handled the situation. I feel very sad and sorry. Not until the events took place did I believe such a thing could happen.' The people felt that the violence in Tiananmen Square startlingly showed that guarantees of freedoms and protection in the Basic Law were worth nothing when the government which pledged them had so little respect for human rights and the rule of law. Many were now convinced that to find a way out of Hong Kong was their best insurance.

Some residents had already felt insecure before June 1989, and now virtually anybody who could afford to do so, or whose skills were welcome in a foreign country, was attempting to gain the right of abode elsewhere. Hong Kong offices buzzed as ashen-faced employees exchanged the latest information on migration rules and shortcuts. Emigration from Hong Kong was nothing new, but the émigrés tended to be the wealthy who acquired foreign passports by making suitably large investments in the host countries and then returned to Hong Kong. A local ditty of the time described the situation succinctly:

The great and the good at the China Club (from left): art dealer Johnson Chang Tsong-zung; Deng Lin, artist and daughter of Deng Xiaoping; Li Ka-shing; Zhou Nan; T. T. Tsui, businessman and art patron; and David Tang

> Those with cash
> Can always dash;
> And for the poor,
> The Basic Law.

After the horrors of 4 June, those whose expertise was most needed to build and run Hong Kong—middle managers, technicians, and professionals—joined the exodus. The numbers leaving Hong Kong each year had hovered around 20,000 in the aftermath of the Joint Declaration in 1984. In 1990, they shot up to 62,000.

The process of emigration is complex, depressing, and expensive. Hong Kong's own term—'spacemen'—for the increasingly common phenomenon of split families, with the husband left working in Hong Kong while the wife and children set up home in a foreign country, notching up the time required to obtain residency—refers to the frequent long-distance flights undertaken by the emigrants. Besides 'spacemen', other new terms peppered conversations in the early 1990s; one was 'serving the emigration jail sentence'. This seemed to show that people really did not want to leave Hong Kong; it was only dread of the future that drove them.

In this charged atmosphere, and under local and international pressure to fulfil its moral obligation to the people of Hong Kong, the British government agreed to break its tight citizenship rules. A British Nationality Scheme was devised whereby passports were offered to 50,000 heads of households after a means test that awarded the most points for qualifications, youth, experience, and participation in public service. Applicants could obtain British passports without meeting residence requirements, a concession that enabled them to remain in Hong Kong. To the dismay of all involved, however, China promptly undermined the point of these special British passports by announcing that they would not be recognized after the handover of sovereignty in 1997. Thus the passports would only be worthwhile if the holders left Hong Kong.

THE HONG KONG STORY

Major-General Bryan Dutton, commander of the British forces in Hong Kong, and the man designated to head the People's Liberation Army garrison after the handover, Major-General Liu Zhenwu

Other efforts to shore up confidence also backfired. Governor Wilson's attempt to persuade China to amend the draft Basic Law (for example, by dropping the provision of stationing a garrison in Hong Kong) made no headway, while his support for the enactment of a Bill of Rights only added to China's distrust of Britain and Hong Kong. Finally promulgated in 1991, the Bill of Rights has come under fire from the Chinese government which has threatened to repeal key sections of it after the transfer of sovereignty. The building of a new airport, which Governor Wilson announced with a fanfare in his policy address in October 1989, was even more controversial. This project, with its associated bridges, tunnels, railway, roads, reclamation, new town, and colossal price tag of $156.4 billion, promised to be the world's largest construction scheme. Experts had long advocated the need for an expanded airport, but this scheme also promised to confer, by opening up the whole of northern Lantau island as a new development area, huge economic benefits. Wilson's announcement that it would go ahead was apparently intended to deflect Hong Kong from dwelling on its immediate troubles and to show faith in its future, but China condemned the project out of hand.

Accusations flew over the thorny issue of financing. Chinese leaders seemed convinced that, in approving such a large expenditure, Britain was actually planning to spend Hong Kong's reserves on work for contract-strapped British construction firms. In blocking the project China had two forms of leverage at hand: first, land could only be released with the agreement of both the present and future sovereign powers, and second, since the project would straddle the handover period, international banks would be reluctant to lend without China's blessing. Nevertheless, the Provisional Airport Authority, set up to mastermind the project, forged ahead with site formation, since further delays would jeopardize the completion date of 1997 set by Governor Wilson.

Lu Ping (left), Director of the Hong Kong and Macau Affairs Office, with Zhou Nan, Director of the New China News Agency, in 1995

In the end, there seemed only one way out of the impasse: Britain had to be more conciliatory towards China. After intensive negotiations, Sir Percy Cradock, foreign affairs advisor to the British prime minister, agreed the terms of a 'memorandum of understanding' on the airport with Lu Ping, Director of the Hong Kong and Macau Affairs Office in China's Foreign Ministry. These terms required the

Hong Kong government to consult China on all the important aspects of the project. Cradock also promised that the prime minister, John Major, would fly to Peking to sign the memorandum with his opposite number, Li Peng. In September 1991 China was still a pariah among nations, and the exercise in 'kowtow' by Major—the first head of government to visit Peking since the suppression in Tiananmen—appeared to be giving support to the widely condemned regime.

It was later suggested that Major deeply regretted the visit, and that he decided to take a tougher line with China as a result. His resolve was probably also encouraged by the outcome of Hong Kong's first direct elections at which a democratic party was given overwhelming support by the electorate. In early 1992, Major replaced David Wilson with Chris Patten as the governor of Hong Kong.

Martin Lee

The democratic party that had won such a convincing victory in September 1991 was led by Martin Lee, now Hong Kong's most prominent advocate of democracy. An established Queen's Counsel, he had joined the Legislative Council in 1985. Later, as one of China's closest informal advisors on the legal aspects of the Joint Declaration, he was appointed to the Basic Law drafting committee. Expelled from this body in 1989 for his support of the student democracy movement in China, he became the main force in the founding of the United Democrats of Hong Kong Party (later known as the Democratic Party). He was particularly vehement in opposing an amendment to Article 23 of the draft Basic Law, which deals with sedition and subversion and which was widely seen as a measure to quell any further support by Hong Kong activists for the democracy movement in China. With Szeto Wah, his fellow campaigner, Lee showed his disapproval by publicly burning a copy of the draft.

The Legislative Council chamber

103

Electoral Reforms

Elections

Under British colonial rule, Hong Kong did not have elections to the Legislative Council (Legco) until 1985. The Joint Declaration promised that the Special Administrative Region 'shall be constituted by elections'. Britain assured Hong Kong that there would be a steady expansion of democracy over the transitional period. It was hoped that a 'through-train' arrangement could be agreed, so that officials and members of Legco would straddle the transfer of sovereignty and continue to serve under the SAR government.

Despite a groundswell of democratic aspirations among Hong Kong people, only cautious and limited steps towards developing representative government in the territory were taken in the late 1980s.

1985 Elections

In 1985, 24 of the 57 members were elected—all indirectly—with twelve seats each from 'functional constituencies' and an 'election committee'. Functional constituencies were occupational groups, such as the professions, trade unions, and financial institutions, which elected one of their number to sit on Legco. The election committee was drawn from members of local authorities—the district boards and municipal councils. Of the remainder, 22 were 'unofficial' members (prominent public figures) and ten were 'official' (civil servants)—appointed by the governor who, as President of Legco, was a member of the council himself.

1991 Elections

In 1991 the elective component was expanded to a majority of seats on Legco. For the first time there were members directly elected from 18 geographical constituencies. The number of functional seats was also increased, while the 'official' seats were cut back.

1995 Elections

The Basic Law stipulated that in the 1995 election the number of members directly elected from geographical constituencies would rise from 18 to 20, and the functional seats from 21 to 30. Thereafter, the geographical seats would increase in successive steps until the year 2007, when all Legco seats (a total of 60) could be elected. 'The ultimate aim', Article 68 pledged, 'is the election of all the members of the Legislative Council by universal suffrage'.

The Last Governor

Governor and Mrs Patten

Less than a year after the elections, Chris Patten, the twenty-eighth and last British colonial governor, arrived to take up his post in Hong Kong. Dispensing with such gubernatorial trappings as plumed hat and sword, Patten settled rapidly and energetically into office. A former senior minister of the British government and close friend of John Major, Patten was a man of far more political weight and experience than any previous governor. Although, as chairman of the Conservative Party, he had contributed significantly to the Tory election victory in April 1992, he had lost his own seat as a Member of Parliament. People in Hong Kong initially saw him as a failed politician and the governorship as his consolation prize.

Ellen Li, 87-year-old feminist and former Legco member:

'One thing that the British did very well in Hong Kong—they gave us a good steady government so that we can work and live here peacefully, and we appreciate that very much.'

The sitting room at Government House

Patten's style was immediately apparent in the dynamic way he presented his first policy address on 7 October 1992. Entitled 'Our Next Five Years', it was an agenda for a comprehensive social welfare programme and, more importantly, for a more 'accountable government'. The pace of democratization was constrained, he admitted, but 'not stopped dead in its tracks'. To achieve a greater measure of popular representation for Hong Kong he proposed a package of electoral reforms which maximized every inch of room for manoeuvre in the Basic Law. 'What I have tried to do with these proposals', Patten explained, 'is to meet two objectives which I understand represent the views of the community . . . to extend democracy while working with the Basic Law.'

His speech delivered, the governor moved straight into a tightly packed, unprecedentedly direct programme of selling his policies to the public. Over the next few days he took part in numerous forums, phone-ins, and interviews with the local and world media.

Patten's proposals caused an instant stir. There was excitement in the liberal camp but dismay and outrage among the pro-China groups. The latter thought the spirit of the Basic Law had been infringed, though they were hard put to pinpoint where the letter was violated. The New China News Agency immediately branded the proposals as 'grossly irresponsible'. The governor was unrepentant: 'What I am trying to do in Hong Kong is an important adventure,' he assured a local magazine, 'a commitment to a system of values.' The result of the ensuing political row between China and Britain was to place Hong Kong higher in the consciousness of the world, further fuelling the irritation of Peking.

Some two weeks after the speech, Patten made his one and only trip as governor to Peking. China's coolness was obvious from the moment he stepped down from the plane at Capital Airport: no high-ranking officials were lined up there to receive him. The most senior official he met during his stay was Foreign Minister Qian Qichen. A *Far Eastern Economic Review* editorial entitled 'John Bull in a China Shop' put both the visit and China's outrage at Patten's proposals into historical perspective by comparing the governor to an eighteenth-century British envoy: 'Not since Lord Macartney refused to get down on all fours . . . has a British manoeuvre so unsettled Peking.'

China's misgivings about British intentions for Hong Kong seemed justified when a secret exchange of letters between the two countries, dating from 1989 and 1990, was published on the governor's return from Peking. These letters revealed that Britain had

Government House

Patten's Proposals

Patten knew that for the last election under British rule he could not increase the number of elected seats without breaching the Basic Law. On the other hand, he could search for 'elbow room', as he called it, in the absence of a definition of the voting base, to develop Hong Kong's representative institutions to the maximum extent.

His main proposals were:

- That the franchise in the existing 21 functional constituencies—covering sectors of the economy— should be extended to individual company directors. Previously the vote was in effect just exercised by the head of the organization. A further nine new functional constituencies were due to be created under the Basic Law, but the detailed arrangements were not specified. Patten suggested that they should cover the entire working population of 2.7 million, divided by occupation, effectively giving every worker a vote at the work place, in addition to his or her vote in the geographical constituency.
- That the number of directly elected members for the geographical constituencies should remain at 20, but that the system should be made simpler by changing the voting system to a single vote for a single seat, and by redrawing constituency boundaries. (At the 1991 election each elector cast two votes, and the first two candidates past the post in a constituency joined Legco.)
- That the election committee would draw all or most of its members from the district boards which were to be re-organized to consist of members who had themselves been directly elected.
- That the voting age should be lowered from 21 to 18 (the same as in China).
- That overlapping membership of the Executive Council and the Legislative Council would be abolished in order 'to make the former a non-party political body' to which he, the governor, could look for 'impartial advice'.

On 29 June 1994, after an 18-hour debate, the electoral reforms bill passed on to the statute book. China announced that they would be revoked immediately after the handover.

Hari Harilela, Honorary President of the Scout Association (Hong Kong Branch), with Governor Sir Edward Youde, the Chief Scout of Hong Kong, at the Annual St. George's Day Rally and Awards Ceremony, 1983

apparently agreed to formulas relating to the composition of Legco. However, as it was subsequently reported, the Foreign and Commonwealth Office had failed to disclose this agreement to Patten. The furore this aroused only added to the disquiet felt by many people in Hong Kong, and the community became increasingly divided. Whereas Patten's reform package had won plaudits at first, a poll published a mere seventeen days after the policy speech claimed that, of those asked, 48 per cent believed that he should abandon it in the face of the Chinese government's unsettling reaction. 'Governor faces loss of support', was the bold headline of one Sunday paper. Hari Harilela, speaking as head of the Indian community, echoed the thinking of many a conservative magnate when he said, 'In upsetting the Chinese, the proposals will upset a smooth transition and the "through-train".'

The political row rumbled on with the Chinese authorities continually increasing local anxieties and chipping away at the more pragmatic edge of Patten's support. The airport was still not really assured, although site preparation work continued. Other major infrastructure projects came under risk. Jardine's tender for a new container terminal was blocked because the hong was thought by China to be guilty of supporting Patten, among its other sins.

Meanwhile the China camp was busy shoring up its support and setting up what was to all intents and purposes a shadow government. In 1993, when Sino-British relations had all but broken down, the so-called Preliminary Working Committee was formed to tackle arrangements in the transitional period, pre-empting the brief of the Joint Liaison Group.

Legco passed Patten's political reforms in 1994. A year or so later the Preliminary Working Committee gave way to a Preparatory Committee of Hong Kong and mainland Chinese delegates, which was given the responsibility of laying the foundations for the post-handover government and legislature. This group was provided for in the Basic Law; it was not, however, in session until eighteen months before the transfer of sovereignty.

Countdown

Despite the political turbulence, Hong Kong's economy thrived. It is a paradox of Hong Kong in its last years as a British colony that its economy should have performed so well in a climate of political uncertainty, argument, and recrimination. During this period Patten moved ahead on the promised improvements to social welfare services. Funding for these was always supplemented by generous donations from the Jockey Club (which funnels its considerable income from betting to a variety of charities), but it was increasingly felt that prosperous Hong Kong could well afford a better and more

Tsing Ma Bridge

comprehensive level of welfare. Meanwhile, a very high rate of employment was assured with constant infrastructural improvements and construction of the new airport (including the magnificent Tsing Ma suspension bridge, the longest road and rail bridge in the world). An ironic twist to history was provided when in the early 1990s Hong Kong became a destination for economic refugees from recession-bound Britain and elsewhere. While nervous local residents packed their bags, workers and job-seekers from the United States, Britain, Canada, and Australia came pouring in. A proportion of the incoming nationals were in fact Hong Kong Chinese returning with their foreign passports secured. They and other newly arrived expatriates had come flocking to Hong Kong because there were more economic opportunities and better prospects in the territory than the countries they had left behind.

Dining room in the China Club

It is not hard to see why this was so. A newspaper headline announced exultantly one morning in 1992: 'We're Richer than the UK!', for in that year Hong Kong's per capita gross domestic product overtook that of Britain. For those seeking other signs of reversal, a moment of high symbolism might have been discerned in the opening, in 1991, of the China Club, which nudged the Hong Kong Club off its lofty perch as 'the paradise of the select and temple of colonial gentility'. Its opening ceremony, orchestrated by the flamboyant businessman David Tang, was also a sign of the times, for it was performed by Zhou Nan, head of the New China News Agency, and in the presence of British cabinet minister Michael Heseltine.

Remembrance Day 1996; among those who attended were the heads of Hong Kong's leading companies and hongs, including Alasdair Morrison, the incumbent taipan of Jardine's (far left). Jack Edwards, veteran and champion of British citizenship for war widows, shows off his medals

Other subtle changes were becoming apparent. Perhaps inevitably, colonial nostalgia pervaded Hong Kong as June 1997 approached; many who attended the Remembrance Day ceremony in November 1996—the last under the British flag—were more than normally sombre when the last post was sounded. In government, a localization policy had ensured that the top officials were now all to be Chinese. In business, as we saw in Chapter 5, Chinese entrepreneurs had begun to annex the power of the European hongs. A further development of this changing order was the appearance of would-be taipans from mainland China, and no-one exemplified this shift better than Rong Zhijian (son of the Shanghai textile industrialist, Rong Yiren, who bucked the trend and did not move to Hong Kong in 1949). Also known as Larry Yung, this 'red capitalist' heads China International Trust and Investment Corporation (CITIC), a Chinese state-owned enterprise with ministry status set up in 1980 as the country's foreign investment vehicle. It is a highly diversified and lucrative conglomerate with stakes—alongside Swire's—in Hong Kong's airline, Cathay Pacific, as well as interests in utilities, property, a merchant bank, and various international firms. Not only is he rich and powerful enough to challenge the old hong establishment, but Larry Yung has also usurped the Jockey Club stewardship traditionally reserved for the taipan of Jardine's. Not surprisingly for someone of his background, he plays the part of taipan extremely well; but more curious perhaps is his taste for things English. His penchant for racing apart, he treats his guests at the stewards' box to the finest clarets; and for relaxation he spends time at his English country house, Birch Grove in Sussex, once the home of British prime minister Harold Macmillan.

Though chairman of a Chinese enterprise, Yung was nevertheless outspoken against any attempt by Peking to interfere in Hong

Swire chairman, Peter Sutch, who has guided the hong towards greater co-operation with mainland Chinese businesses

Larry Yung leading his horse at a race meeting, 1996

Kong after the handover. He also warned the people of Hong Kong not to bend over backwards to accommodate Peking's wishes.

The crucial test facing the man who will replace Chris Patten to govern Hong Kong after the handover is whether he will be able to stand up to Peking. On 12 December 1996 the future Chief Executive, the replacement governor, was voted in by 400 electors who were themselves hand-picked behind closed doors in Peking. The man chosen was Tung Chee-hwa (C. H. Tung), a 59-year-old shipping magnate and businessman. Son of C. Y. Tung, who was part of the Shanghai exodus in the late

The four candidates for the post of Chief Executive, Hong Kong SAR, photographed before the selection of Tung Chee-hwa was confirmed (from left): Peter Woo Kwong-ching, Simon Li Fook-sean, Sir T. L. Yang, and Tung Chee-hwa

1940s, Chee-hwa had arrived in Hong Kong as a child. After school in Hong Kong, he attended Liverpool University in Britain and spent some years working in the United States. Tung Chee-hwa has said in interviews that Hong Kong must maintain its 'rule of law, an independent judiciary, efficient civil service, conservative fiscal policies, a level playing field'. He told journalists that he respected Western values but admired, even more, the Asian tendency to emphasize obligations rather than rights. Hong Kong's strength, he believed, was its 'ability to absorb what is good about the West and what is good about Chinese culture'.

The Hong Kong that Tung will take over is an amazing phenomenon by any count. From its beginnings as a barren rock, Hong Kong is now the world's eighth largest trading economy, tenth largest exporter of services, and fourth largest banking centre and foreign exchange market, with the busiest container port and the third busiest airport. Its population of six million enjoys a higher standard of living than the citizens of several European nations. It

Container port

Publicity stunt or political statement? A protester anticipated the end of British rule in Hong Kong by smearing the statue of Queen Victoria with red paint in 1996

has virtually full employment, one of the lowest crime rates of any city, an efficient civil service, and a trusted judiciary. In 1995 an American research institute, the Heritage Foundation, judged it the freest economy out of 140 contenders.

Will all this change when one of the freest economies returns to the rule of the largest totalitarian state in the world? They will make strange partners, sharing the same bed but dreaming different dreams, as the Chinese idiom (*tong chuang yi meng*) has it. Or will they? As might be expected, a wide spectrum of opinions is being tendered, by experts and laymen alike, during the countdown to 1 July 1997. The pessimists feel that the special combination of Britishness and Chineseness which has made Hong Kong's story so successful is too fragile to last. They dismiss the attempts of the last decade to entrench democracy and human rights as futile, since China will not lack means to influence voters or exert control anyway. They are sure that corruption and oppression will take over.

The optimists see the choice of Tung Chee-hwa as Chief Executive of the SAR as a sign that China will preserve Hong Kong's capitalist system and encourage the growth of business. Hong Kong, they say, has to be viewed in the context of the East Asian economic miracle, which, after all, also includes China. Hong Kong is the main destination for China's exports and by far her largest source of foreign investment; China will not carelessly sacrifice the well-being of this golden goose. By forfeiting a degree of democracy to keep its economic freedom now, Hong Kong may yet survive as a successful trading and financial centre until China herself becomes more open and less authoritarian. People need only point to the transformation of China in the last fifteen years, the optimists say, to feel hopeful that the next generation in power will continue to move slowly but surely along the path of reform. If Hong Kong is then swept up in this march towards prosperity, its story is perhaps only just beginning.

The last word must, however, belong to those whose personal and family chronicles have formed part of the Hong Kong story.

Eric Hotung, grandson of Sir Robert Hotung and special advisor on Chinese affairs to the Georgetown Center for International

Mr and Mrs Eric Hotung

Members of the British Chamber of Commerce firing Jardine's noonday gun. The gun will continue to be fired after 1 July 1997

Strategic Studies in Washington, said in 1988, 'I am convinced that the leadership in Beijing wants to preserve and nourish the incomparable qualities that are the basis of Hong Kong's amazing productiveness. In the inevitable climate of uncertainty as the deadline of 1997 approaches, the people of Hong Kong can take encouragement in the thought that neither China nor Great Britain can afford to be anything less than fair and generous.' He added, in late 1996, that he still held to this view.

The taipan of Jardine's, Alasdair Morrison, in an address to the Hong Kong General Chamber of Commerce in January 1995, came close to deploring the hong's anti-China image: 'Plainly some of Jardine's actions have caused offence in China in recent years. That is a matter of regret to us. . . . There will be no group in Hong Kong, whether before or after 1997, which has a greater interest than Jardine Matheson in a stable and prosperous Hong Kong and in a straightforward, open, and sincere relationship with China.'

John Shoemaker, American businessman and long-time resident of Hong Kong, was optimistic about the Hong Kong's economic future in late 1996: 'The big transition for Hong Kong is the return to China on 30th June 1997. Although this is a set date, the actual process has been long underway and we expect the handover itself to be about as momentous as the sun finally setting on the British empire. Hardly a great revelation! What it does mean is that a lot of attention is going to be focused on Hong Kong and China, and we think investors will like what they see. Both markets look attractive from a cyclical standpoint, and what we basically have is the unique situation of one of the world's great emerging markets in China, positioned right

The new symbol of the Hong Kong Special Administrative Region

111

William Tang

*Abandoned village in the Pat Sin Leng
Country Park, New Territories*

next to a city that has twenty-first-century infrastructure and a fully serviced economy. We've already started to see the markets taking off and we continue to believe that it's the best investment story in the region.'

In a filmed interview in 1996, C. C. Lee, textile manufacturer, said: 'What happens in Hong Kong will affect the economy of China. China needs Hong Kong, but Hong Kong needs China also. I am confident that the Peking government wants Hong Kong to succeed.'

William Tang, fashion designer, is a descendant of the first Tang settlers in the New Territories. He travels regularly between London and Hong Kong and maintains the 300-year-old family house in Yuen Long which was passed to him by his father. He admitted in an interview in 1996 that he had mixed feelings about the change of sovereignty: 'It's been a struggle in my mind but in the last couple of years I have thought about it in a more objective and reasonable way. I believe I need to be in a place which I can call home, a place that I can always come back to. So now I don't worry about the 1997 issue any more. If the worst comes to the worst and the situation becomes very bad I will just stay quietly in my village—at least I'm home.'

'I don't feel nervous about the future,' said Hari Harilela in 1996. 'I think Hong Kong is going to be good for the next five years. I think that business is going to be good, as long as we believe that China won't interfere more that it does today. "One country–two systems". So far so good. China has been very fair, according to the Basic Law. I have made several trips to Beijing—I'm an advisor to the Chinese government—and I know the present leaders are very sincere that we should stay put. They don't want to lose face that, after the British left, they couldn't control the trade and commerce.'

Shanghai-born Michael Green, leader of the Jewish community, wrote in an article published by the *South China Morning Post* in 1996: 'Some of the leading industries in the world are run by

Jimmy Lai featured in an advertising campaign on his debut as publisher of the Chinese-language newspaper, Apple Daily

Asians, so why is it there has been a gradual downgrading of talent in Hong Kong, which has exposed us to the dubious fortunes of being left in the hands of tired, end-of-tour functionaries who have sought not to rock the boat? . . . In Hong Kong, the best is yet to come. . . . What Hong Kong essentially needs is a little less whining about the so-called economic and political uncertainties linked to the handover, and in its place a little more honest scrutiny of what could have been done, and still can be done, to put Hong Kong back at the forefront of Asia's most dynamic economies where we belong.'

Garment-manufacturer-turned-publisher Jimmy Lai Chee-ying has been an audacious critic of the Chinese leadership, particularly through the columns of his Chinese-language newspaper, *Apple Daily*. He said in an interview in early 1996, 'If Hong Kong stands firm and fights, then we will have a strong chance of autonomy. If we let [the mainland Chinese] run Hong Kong, no matter how sincere they are, they won't know how to run it. All we have to do is to try to uphold the freedoms we have.'

Jack Tang was one of the Shanghainese garment manufacturers who came to Hong Kong in the 1950s: 'I guess forty years is a long time in Hong Kong. I guess all my business experience has been in Hong Kong. But I don't feel I have real roots. I like to see myself as sort of worldly. I enjoy myself anywhere I go. I like all the places I've been to and I travel a lot, but Hong Kong is still of course closer to my heart than any other place.'

Zhou Nan, Director of the New China News Agency in Hong Kong, delivered a China National Day message on 1 October 1996. Here are some extracts:

'In fewer than 300 days, Hong Kong will end its history under British occupation and return to the embrace of its motherland. This is a momentous event in the history of the Chinese nation and will be the focus of worldwide attention. In this sense, celebrating our National Day shortly before China resumes its exercise of sovereignty over Hong Kong is of extraordinary significance. . . .

The fundamentals of Hong Kong's economy are stable and healthy . . . the economy will stage a moderate rebound, with the growth rate standing at last year's level or a bit higher. There has been continuous inflow of external capital from other countries in recent years. According to statistics in mid-1996, Hong Kong hosts representative offices for 4,523 foreign companies, among which about 40 per cent were opened in the past five years. Surveys by several foreign chambers of commerce show that at least 95 per cent of foreign businessmen will not only continue to develop in Hong Kong but also plan to enlarge their staff numbers to expand their business after 1997.

External capital inflow continues to grow, as does the number of returnees. This has provided ample evidence of people's full confidence in the future of Hong Kong. . . .

Of course, there are some people who do not wish to see a smooth transition in Hong Kong and who have always tried to disrupt the smooth transition by making noise and trouble. Yet the mainstream of Hong Kong society stands for stability not turbulence, co-operation not confrontation, and smooth transition not disturbance. This is where our common aspirations and common interests lie. Hong Kong's recovery is a significant event, for which people of Chinese descent around the world have long aspired. . . . I am convinced that with the great motherland as a powerful backing . . . we can . . . maintain Hong Kong's long-term stability and prosperity . . . and make sure the "Pearl of the Orient" will glitter even more brightly.'

One year closer to the handover—the chairman of the Hongkong and Shanghai Bank, Sir William Purves, who masterminded the move of the Bank's headquarters to London from Hong Kong in 1993, dancing with Lady Purves after the midnight firing of the noonday gun at New Year 1992. Nigel Rich, Jardine's taipan at the time, is on her left

Countdown to Hong Kong's reversion of sovereignty, in Tiananmen Square

Gerry Forsgate, businessman and former chairman of the Urban Council, spoke about the future in a 1997 interview: 'This is no place for retired gentlemen. You get knocked over by people on the pavement. You've got to be able to continue to pick up the pace. If you no longer want to go at the pace, then you really have to leave Hong Kong. . . . I like Hong Kong. I'm interested in what's happening. I have a great deal of faith in C. H. Tung—I've known him for many years, and I think that the team he will put together will do a good job for Hong Kong.'

Lady Lobo, a Eurasian married to Sir Roger Lobo (former member of the

Governor Patten and Zhou Nan at a ceremony marking China's national day, 1995

Executive Council), and sister of Andrew Choa, is equally positive about the future: 'I'm not in the least nervous. My husband Roger and I are not nervous at all. Ever since the signing of the Joint Declaration in 1984 we decided we are for Hong Kong. He's worked for the Hong Kong community for the last fifty years and he's very dedicated to Hong Kong and we both love Hong Kong, so we don't intend to go anywhere at all and we are very, very hopeful. Of course there will be changes, and some very irritating things might happen, but there is no danger. So long as there's freedom of religion, freedom to travel, freedom of the judiciary, we're happy to stay.'

Martin Lee wrote, at the end of 1996, in one of Australia's leading journals, *The Age*: 'If China is allowed to switch off the lights in Hong Kong, darkness will fall not only on Hong Kong and China, but across the entire Asia-Pacific region. This need not happen. We in Hong Kong are committed to staying and fighting to keep Hong Kong free.'

Governor Chris Patten gave his swansong policy address on 2 October 1996:

'Governors have lived for Hong Kong. One or two have literally died for Hong Kong. But all have found Hong Kong, in and out of office, an all-consuming interest. Retired to our grey and green island, past governors have watched from afar with keen-eyed interest and, doubtless, occasional frustration as Hong Kong's history has unfolded. I shall do the same, carrying with me one frustration, gnawed by one anxiety, comforted by one certainty.

For me the frustration, the greatest in this job, is that I have not been able to put my personal view of Hong Kong's best interests to the test which legitimizes leadership in most free societies: the test of the ballot box. But Hong Kong has been promised that its government will develop so that the ballot box can happen one day—a day I hope I shall see, and a day that I shall be delighted to put down to China's credit and to the credit of those in this territory who have stood up bravely for the people of Hong Kong.

My anxiety is this: not that this community's autonomy would be usurped by Peking, but that it could be given away bit by bit by some people in Hong Kong. We all know that over the last couple of years we have seen decisions, taken in good faith by the Government of Hong Kong, appealed surreptitiously to Peking; decisions taken in the interests of the whole community lobbied against behind closed doors by those whose personal interests may have been adversely affected. That is damaging to Hong Kong because it draws Chinese officials into matters which should fall squarely within the autonomy of Hong Kong. If we in Hong Kong want our autonomy, then it needs to be defended and asserted by everyone here—by businessmen, politicians, journalists, academics, and other community leaders, as well as by public servants.

And what of that truth which more than anything else gives me confidence in Hong Kong? The truth is this. The qualities, the beliefs, the ideals that have made Hong Kong's present will still be here to shape Hong Kong's future.

Hong Kong, it seems to me, has always lived by the author, Jack London's, credo:

I would rather be ashes than dust,
I would rather my spark should burn out in a
    brilliant blaze.
Than it should be stifled in dry rot.
I would rather be a superb meteor,
With every atom of me in magnificent glow,
Than a sleepy and permanent planet.

Whatever the challenges ahead, nothing should bring this meteor crashing to earth, nothing should snuff out its glow. I hope that Hong Kong will take tomorrow by storm.

And when it does, history will stand and cheer.'

CHAPTER 7

Chris Patten: Valedictory

W hat's the best view in Hong Kong, the one that most indelibly prints the essence, the very nature of Hong Kong on your memory?

Is it the view from the Star Ferry on a fine day as you buck and weave your way across the harbour, looking up at the Peak and the skyscrapers—those side-by-side tributes to God and mammon?

Or is it the view from the top of the Dragon's Back—Shek O and its silver beaches below, and the deep green hilltops folding and unfolding ahead of you?

Or maybe you prefer Sai Kung, Double Haven, the Lantau Buddha; or any market scene with the red light shades, the exotic fruit, the fish in tanks, the hens in wicker cages; or the window of your favourite baker's; or the back of the shop in any ironmonger's?

Well, there's no shortage of choices. But high up on everyone's list must surely come the spectacle of race night at Happy Valley; Hong Kongers enjoying themselves, doing one of the things they like best. Every visitor I've ever taken to Happy Valley has come away just as excited as I'd told them they would be. The first time my sister came to Hong Kong, she went virtually straight from the plane to the race track. She's never forgotten that initial overwhelming sight. There's literally nothing like it in the world.

Wan Chai and Hong Kong's tallest building, Central Plaza

A traditional medicine shop

117

Tram stop, Des Voeux Road in Central district

The crowd and the bustle as dusk closes in and the lights around the track up and down the sides of the valley and on the passing double-decker buses blaze across the sky. The yellows and greens and reds of the jockeys and the swagger and polish of trainers. The excitement of the races themselves—flashing boards with their incomprehensible mathematical messages to the betting faithful, a squadron of galloping horses cresting the last bend and hitting the gallop for home, the sound of the hooves and the roar of the crowd and the whoosh of relief when it's all over, and the bouquets and the silver trophies and the bigwigs from the Jockey Club in the winners' enclosure.

Hong Kong, you will gather, is a very special place. Its history is one of the most remarkable in our century. While some may choose to view it through the story of the Opium War and the humiliations inflicted by the imperial powers on the Qing dynasty, for most of Hong Kong's residents the history lessons are of more recent vintage. The great majority of Hong Kongers are themselves refugees, or the family of refugees, from the turbulent events of China's recent past. They escaped the war with Japan, the fighting between com-

A cemetery between Lo Wu (on the Hong Kong side of the border) and Shenzhen (the Special Economic Zone in China)

Bird fanciers in Kowloon

munists and the Nationalists, the communist take-over, the expropriation of their property and assets in Shanghai, the starvation years of the Great Leap Forward, the reckless cruelties of the Cultural Revolution. They swam. They crawled. They ran. They climbed. They came to Hong Kong with nothing, to a city which had little except the laws and the customs which give men and women the chance to live in peace and freedom, to thrive and excel. And excel they did.

The prosperity they have created is extraordinary. The first time we calculated our gross domestic product was in 1961. Then it was US$0.897 billion. Today it is US$142.44 billion—21 per cent of China's, though our population is only 0.5 per cent of China's. The first time we calculated our gross domestic product per head was in 1961. Then it was US$410. Today it is US$25,000. Hong Kong is the eighth largest trading community in the world. We have the seventh largest financial reserves, the eighth largest stock market with a capitalization of US$304 billion, and we are the fifth largest centre for foreign exchange dealing. We have the world's busiest port and the third busiest airport. We are building what will be the second busiest airport.

With economic development has gone social progress. We have built nearly a million flats to house those who once lived in squatter huts. Where once there was epidemic disease, now we have health statistics which stand comparison with any in the OECD countries. Only Japan boasts longer life expectancy for its people. Our child mortality statistics are better than Germany's, America's, and—dare I say it—Britain's. A decade ago, 3 per cent of our young people went into tertiary education. Today one in four do so, three-quarters of them to study for degrees, the rest for other forms of qualification. Nearly half of those who graduated in 1995 came from public housing estates, and only 12 per cent had parents who had advanced beyond secondary education. It has been a real social revolution.

Public housing in Hong Kong, late 1980s

The statistics are impressive. But statistics are only half the story. Statistics need to be fleshed out. I find my thoughts drawn back often to two very personal moments. One was shortly after my arrival as governor here in 1992, when I was finding out about welfare services. On a hot, wet day in July I had been to a rehabilitation centre, and emerged to find a number of parents of handicapped children waiting in the rain to petition me. I was struck by their patience, by the moderation of their requests compared to the difficulties they faced, by their love and concern for their children. Those are qualities that I have met time and time again here. The moderation, particularly in politics, is remarkable given the extraordinary changes that Hong Kong has experienced and is going through. The second event was more traumatic, seeing the families of those who had died or been injured in the terrible fire in November 1996 in the Garley Building— poor people devastated by the loss of

Lunch break in Woosung Street, Yau Ma Tei, Kowloon

119

The last colonial Christmas . . . Chris and Lavender Patten with their daughters Kate, Laura, and Alice

children, brothers, sisters. It was a salutary reminder that while the boosters of Hong Kong, myself included, often talk about how prosperous this city has become, many of Hong Kong's citizens have not yet attained a level of opulence, that their hopes for the future are not founded on financial resources but on prospects for their sons and daughters, on the exchanges and satisfactions of family life.

But hopes they certainly have. Because one of the most striking things about this community is its hope and faith in the future. People assume that their lives will get better, and go on getting better. That tomorrow will be better than today.

That they have such faith says a lot about Hong Kong and about the way it runs its affairs. Economic opportunity has been indispensable to Hong Kong, but without freedom and ability to take and to create that opportunity it would have meant little. Investment in education has been of greater importance than equities, while civil liberties have become inextricably linked with the success of the economic liberties this city enjoys.

Some months ago I opened an excellent exhibition about Hong Kong's past, its present, and its potential future. Of all the exhibits, one made a particularly strong visual impact on me. It was a blown-up photograph of the narrow end of a Mark I housing block, with the

Taoist priest reading prayers during a Ta Chiu festival in Shek O, Hong Kong island

New year flower stall in Victoria Park, Hong Kong

Chinese New Year celebrations, Wong Tai Sin, Kowloon

Vegetable hawker, Kowloon

landings packed with people. Apparently, it was shot in Wong Tai Sin in 1965 during Chinese New Year. The people were all looking down towards the street as a parade of lion dancers went past.

It's a very striking photo. Full of action, and laughter, and the evidence which social history draws on. The poor clothing. The rough, unfinished cement on the walls. The graffiti—far more than you'd see in a housing estate today. The cheerful sense of community solidarity—working people and their families taken out of themselves for a moment by some happy spectacle.

The people in the photo are every age, from grandparents to babes in arms. They are not rich, that's for sure. They are city strivers, street sharp, I'd imagine, and they probably needed to be to survive and prosper in a tougher economic climate.

So what would have concerned them? What would they have worried about? Rice bowl issues I'd guess. Their welfare. The roof over their heads: was it now safe from fire and landslip? How could they fit granny into the flat? What chance of the kids getting secondary education? How to deal with that hacking cough they'd had for years? Would they get a wage rise this year for making more plastic flowers and toys? Would it be possible to get a place on the bus for an outing to the beach at the weekend?

I doubt whether many of them worried much about the subjects which seem to cause so much controversy in Hong Kong these days—freedom of speech, the rule of law, accountable government. Life was a bit more basic. It tends to be the case everywhere that

122

Wong Tai Sin housing block, Chinese New Year, 1965

Cobbler on Canton Road, Kowloon

economic and social development creates its own political agenda. Look elsewhere in Asia. And I suppose that 1997 contributes to this process, too.

Most of the people in that photo must still be alive. Not all of them, of course, will be in Hong Kong. Some will have emigrated. But I should think the majority are still here. And still worrying about welfare issues.

But those issues will have changed a bit. How to afford to buy a flat here on the sort of income which would make it pretty straightforward in a lot of other places? How to get granny into a specially built flat of her own or even a care and attention home? How to get retrained to move from a factory job to an office one? How to brush up your English or Mandarin? How to help your student children pay their way through college? Can you manage a holiday in Malaysia this year, or a trip to visit relatives in the States?

Naturally, there are still some basic needs which have to be met. But as absolute standards have risen for nearly everyone, the social agenda has become more complicated and more sophisticated.

The people in the photo are likely overall to have rather different concerns and worries than they had all those years ago. That's because of what I mentioned earlier—the politics of progress, as well, of course, as the imminent transfer of sovereignty and the questions it raises.

Boats in Stanley, on the south side of Hong Kong island

So, people ask me, are you optimistic about Hong Kong's future? When I try to answer that question honestly I am sometimes accused of being like Voltaire's Dr Pangloss—incurably optimistic, hoping for the best in the best of all possible worlds. Sometimes, though saying exactly the same things, I am said to be like Hecuba's daughter Cassandra, predicting doom. Maybe I should rest my case on what we do in the present to govern Hong Kong well, and leave the future to speak for itself. But I don't think that goes quite far enough. So let me sketch for you briefly why I am—to borrow from the *New York Times*—'warily optimistic'.

First, I'm optimistic because it is so massively in China's interest that things should go well. China must surely recognize that

Nam Chung valley and Robin's Nest, Pat Sin Leng Country Park, New Territories

continued success in China's richest city, its bridge to the world, the source of most of its inward investment, and the target for most of its outward reinvestment, is crucial to the future well-being of China. Most of the major issues that China will face in the next few years will be easier to tackle if the transition goes well in Hong Kong and more difficult if it does not. There is also a good deal of 'face' in China demonstrating to the world that it can manage Hong Kong as well as it has managed the opening of its economy over the last decade and a half; that it can oversee the well-being of Hong Kong as successfully as, or more successfully than, the departing colonial power.

My second reason for optimism lies in the character of the Hong Kong people. Analysis of Hong Kong's future very often takes place as though the people who have made Hong Kong all that it is didn't actually exist. They are somehow written out of the script.

But what can we say with certainty about them? They identify themselves with Hong Kong; they are proud of their city and of what they have achieved. They have developed the infrastructure of civil society in Hong Kong, helping to turn it from a closed, colonial society into an open, international city. Their civic consciousness is not going to be turned off like a light switch at midnight on 30 June 1997. They will remain committed to participating in the running of their own community, to the development of autonomous institutions of a free society—Burke's 'little platoons'. Those who reflect their political aspirations today will almost certainly continue to do so. The advocacy of liberty is not going to be snuffed out.

And one other thing. Is the sort of place Hong Kong has become, are the values which have shaped it, a throw-back to an outdated past in Asia, or a forerunner of what the future will be like in more

Tram in Wan Chai

125

An anomaly created by the 1898 lease was the Kowloon Walled City, which did not recognize British jurisdiction. The area became a fetid slum of illegal structures, and the haunt—it was widely believed—of squatters, criminals, and drug addicts. They began to be moved out in advance of demolition in the late 1980s, and the area is now a park

Vietnamese refugees in a closed camp. Screenings were introduced from 1988 to determine whether they were genuine political refugees or economic migrants. In early 1997 Hong Kong still had several thousand of them awaiting resettlement in third countries, repatriation, or deportation

and more Asian countries? I have no doubt that in Asia as elsewhere the future is in the hands of those who can best combine political liberty and economic freedom.

It is Britain's last major colonial task to do all it can to ensure that Hong Kong has the best possible chance of combining those things in the future. To do what is right is to do what is the right thing for Hong Kong. Neither the present nor the future would have judged us kindly if we had failed to recognize that.

When the sun sets for the last time on the Union flag in Hong Kong in June, when the last note of 'Highland Cathedral' dies on a hot evening wind, when a member of the House of Windsor waves a royal and nautical farewell to a crowd of newly confirmed citizens of the People's Republic of China, it will not literally be the end of the British Empire. There are other colonies scattered across the seas, other plumed hats and Letters Patent, other dependencies where the common law rules and where many Hong Kong firms have now made their legal home.

No literal end of Empire, then. But for most observers, it will look like the real end of the story—a last chapter curiously delayed by historical accident and, because, too, of the dictates of history, a chapter drafted in different terms to its predecessors. Shall we be able in the middle of that summer night to claim, in the words of Jan Morris, that we have made 'a proud valediction to a tremendous historical adventure?'

The handover in June will not be a time for British triumphalism. Nor the occasion for boastful self-congratulation. There may still be problems unresolved, worries still uncalmed. But whatever else we feel when we leave, I hope we can honestly say that we did our best and lived up to our ideals in acutely difficult circumstances; that we left with honour not obloquy.

Plover Cove Country Park

Governors and Administrators of Hong Kong

1841	Captain Charles Elliot*		**1912–19**	Sir Francis Henry May
1841–43	Sir Henry Pottinger*		**1919–25**	Sir Reginald Stubbs
1843–44	Sir Henry Pottinger		**1925–30**	Sir Cecil Clementi
1844–48	Sir John Davis		**1930–35**	Sir William Peel
1848–54	Sir George Bonham		**1935–37**	Sir Alexander Caldecott
1854–59	Sir John Bowring		**1937–40**	Sir Geoffry Northcote
1859–65	Sir Hercules Robinson		**1941–47**	Sir Mark Young
1865–66	William Mercer*		**1947–57**	Sir Alexander Grantham
1866–72	Sir Richard Graves Macdonnell		**1958–64**	Sir Robert Black
1872–77	Sir Arthur Kennedy		**1964–71**	Sir David Trench
1877–82	Sir John Pope Hennessy		**1971–82**	Sir Murray Maclehose
1882–83	Sir William Marsh*		**1982–86**	Sir Edward Youde
1883–85	Sir George Bowen		**1987–92**	Sir David Wilson
1885–87	Sir William Marsh*		**1992–97**	Christopher Patten
1887	Major-General N. G. Cameron*			
1887–91	Sir William Des Voeux			
1891	Major-General Digby Barker*			
1891–98	Sir William Robinson		* Administrators	
1898	Major-General W. Black*			
1898–1903	Sir Henry Blake			
1903–04	Sir Francis Henry May*			
1904–07	Sir Matthew Nathan			
1907–12	Sir Frederick Lugard			

Bibliography

Anon, *Pao Yue-kong in Pictures*, Hangzhou: Zhejiang Photographic Press, 1991

Ayer, *Pico, Video Night in Kathmandu . . . and Other Reports from the Not-So-Far East*, New York: Alfred A. Knopf, 1988

Bard, S., *Traders of Hong Kong: Some Foreign Merchant Houses 1841–1899*, Hong Kong: Urban Council, 1993

Basic Law of the Hong Kong Special Administrative Region of the People's Republic of China, The, Hong Kong: Joint Publishing Co. Ltd, 1991

Beeching, Jack, *The Chinese Opium Wars*, New York: Harcourt Brace Jovanovich, 1975

Blyth, Sally and Wotherspoon, Ian, *Hong Kong Remembers*, Hong Kong: Oxford University Press, 1996

Bonavia, David, *Hong Kong 1997: The Final Settlement*, Hong Kong: South China Morning Post, 1983

Bosanquet, David, *Escape Through China*, London: Robert Hale, 1983

Briggs, Tom and Crisswell, Colin N., *Hong Kong's New Territories: A Land Between*, Hong Kong: South China Morning Post, 1980

Cameron, Nigel, *The Hongkong Land Company Ltd: A Brief History*, Hong Kong: The Hongkong Land Company Ltd, 1979

Chan, Anthony B., *Li Ka-shing: Hong Kong's Elusive Billionaire*, Ontario: Macmillan, 1996

Chang Hsin-pao, *Commissioner Lin and the Opium War*, Cambridge: Cambridge University Press, 1974

Coates, Austin, *Whampoa: Ships on the Shore*, Hong Kong: South China Morning Post, 1980

Cottrell, Robert, *The End of Hong Kong: the Secret Diplomacy of Imperial Retreat*, London: John Murray, 1993

Crisswell, Colin N., *The Taipans: Hong Kong's Merchant Princes*, Hong Kong: Oxford University Press, 1982

Dew, Gwen, *Prisoner of the Japs*, New York: Alfred A. Knopf, 1943

Endacott, G. B., *A History of Hong Kong*, Hong Kong: Oxford University Press, 1973

Endacott, G. B. and Birch, A., *Hong Kong Eclipse*, Hong Kong: Oxford University Press, 1978

First Historical Archives of China, The, (*Xianggang Lishi Wenti Dang'an Tulu*), Hong Kong: Joint Publishing Co. Ltd, 1996

Fong, Peter K. W. and Chan Chik, *Home of Yesterday*, Hong Kong: Joint Publishing Co. Ltd, 1993

Gillingham, Paul, *At the Peak*, Hong Kong: Macmillan, 1983

Greenberg, Michael, *British Trade and the Opening of China 1800–42*, Cambridge: Cambridge University Press, 1951

Hall, Peter A., *In the Web*, England: Hurst Village Publishing, 1992

Han Suyin, *A Many-Spendoured Thing*, London: Jonathan Cape, 1952

Hase, P. H. and Sinn, Elizabeth (eds), *Beyond the Metropolis: Villages in Hong Kong*, Hong Kong: Joint Publishing Co. Ltd, 1995

Hayes, James, 'Hong Kong Island Before 1841', *Journal of the Hong Kong Branch of the Royal Asiatic Society*, 24 (1984)

Hutcheon, Robin, *A Burst of Crackers: The Li & Fung Story*, Hong Kong: Li & Fung, 1992

Hutcheon, Robin, *First Sea Lord: The Life and Work of Sir Y. K. Pao*, Hong Kong: The Chinese University Press, 1990

Hutcheon, Robin, *South China Morning Post: The First Eighty Years*, Hong Kong: South China Morning Post, 1983

Keswick, Maggie (ed.), *The Thistle and the Jade: 150 Years of Jardine Matheson*, London: Octopus Books, 1982

Lethbridge, H. J., *Hongkong: Stability and Change*, Hong Kong: Oxford University Press, 1978

Mason, Richard, *The World of Suzie Wong*, London: Collins, 1957

Mo, Timothy, *Sour Sweet*, London: André Deutsch, 1982

Pope-Hennessy, James, *Half-Crown Colony*, London: Jonathan Cape, 1969

Rafferty, Kevin, *City on the Rocks: Hong Kong's Uncertain Future*, London: Penguin Books, 1991

Roberti, Mark: *The Fall of Hong Kong: China's Triumph and Britain's Betrayal*, New York: John Wiley & Sons, 1994

Sayer, G. R., *Hong Kong 1862–1919: Years of Discretion*, Hong Kong: Hong Kong University Press, 1975

Sinn, Elizabeth, *Growing with Hong Kong: The Bank of East Asia 1919–1994*, Hong Kong: The Bank of East Asia Ltd

Smith, Albert, *To China and Back: Being a Diary Kept, Out and Home*, reprinted Hong Kong: Hong Kong University Press, 1974

Spence, Jonathan D., *The Search for Modern China*, London: Hutchinson, 1990

Tiffany, Jr., Osmond, *The Canton Chinese, or An American's Sojourn in the Celestial Empire*, Boston: James Monroe and Company, 1849

Warner, John, *Hong Kong 100 Years Ago*, Hong Kong: Urban Council, 1970

Waters, Dan, 'The Re-occupation of Hong Kong', *Journal of the Hong Kong Branch of the Royal Asiatic Society*, 31 (1991)

Welsh, Frank, *A History of Hong Kong*, London: HarperCollins Publishers, 1993

White, Barbara-Sue (ed.), *Hong Kong: Somewhere Between Heaven and Earth*, Hong Kong: Oxford University Press, 1996

Wong Siu-lun, *Emigrant Entrepreneurs: Shanghai Industrialists in Hong Kong*, Hong Kong: Oxford University Press, 1988

Picture Credits

Airphoto International: 95

Apple Daily: 113

Robin Baker: 83 (top), 88 (bottom left), 91 (bottom), 96 (top)

Oliver Barnham: endpapers, 22 (top left), 52 (top), 56

Magnus Bartlett: 78, 79 (right), 95

Chan Chik, 61 (right), 62 (bottom), 68 (top right), 69 (bottom), 71 (both), 73 (top), 77

Private collection of Chan Sui-jeung: 25, 36

Roger Cole: 85 (top)

Rogan Coles: 58 (bottom), 108 (top left), 110 (bottom)

The First Historical Archives of China: 2, 10

Greg Gerard: 126 (both)

Government House: 41 (top right), 45 (bottom), 54 (left), 55, 57, 58 (top and centre), 104 (top), 120

Martyn Gregory Gallery: x, 1 (top left), 3 (top), 4 (both), 7 (bottom), 13, 15, 19 (left), 21, 24 (top), 27 (bottom), 29, 31 (top), 32 (top), 34 (bottom)

Hari Harilela: 70, 106

R. A. Y. Herries: 75 (bottom)

The Hongkong and Shanghai Banking Corporation: 6, 7 (top), 8 (top), 17, 53 (top), 59

Hong Kong Government Information Service: 65 (bottom), 66 (top)

The Hong Kong Jockey Club/Ming Yuen Studio: 108 (bottom right)

Hongkong Land: 33 (bottom), 34 (top)

Hong Kong Museum of Art: 11

Hong Kong Museum of History: 5 (bottom), 32 (bottom), 35, 43 (top right), 45 (top), 63 (bottom)

Horstmann & Godfrey Ltd: 43 (left), 46 (top), 50 (top)

Private collection of Eric Hotung: 27 (top), 33 (top), 38, 40 (bottom)

Hu Chui: 9 (bottom), 114 (bottom)

Jardine Matheson: 9 (top two), 87 (right), 109 (bottom), 111 (top), 114 (top)

The late Maggie Keswick Jencks: 39, 42, 44 (both), 46 (bottom), 50 (bottom), 51 (bottom), 52 (bottom), 68 (bottom), 75 (top), 76 (left)

Lady Keswick: 20

Alice King: 67 (top)

Martin Lee: 99, 103 (left)

Li & Fung Ltd: 47 (top)

Li Ka-shing: 91 (top)

Joyce Ma: 89 (bottom)

Adeline Yen Mah: 66 (centre)

Ingrid Morejohn: 100 (top), 118 (top left and centre), 124 (right)

New China News Agency: 60, 76 (bottom), 80, 86, 87 (bottom), 92 (top and bottom), 93 (both), 94 (both), 96 (bottom), 97 (right), 98 (bottom), 100 (right), 102 (both), 111 (bottom right), 115

Peabody and Essex Museum, Salem, Massachusetts: 5 (top)

Brian Pearce: 97 (top left), 112 (left), 117 (all three), 118 (bottom left), 119 (bottom right), 121 (both), 122 (bottom), 124 (top left), 125 (both), 127 (right)

Alan Rees/Mott MacDonald Hong Kong Ltd: 107 (top)

South China Morning Post: 84 (centre and bottom), 85 (bottom), 92 (centre), 109 (top right), 110 (top left)

Andrew Stables: 103 (bottom right), 104 (bottom), 105

John Swire & Sons: 26 (top), 30 (bottom), 41 (bottom), 41 (top left), 53 (bottom), 108 (centre)

Private collection of David Tang: vii, 3 (bottom), 8 (bottom), 14, 18, 24 (bottom), 28 (top), 37, 47 (bottom), 49 (both), 101, 107 (bottom right)

William Tang: 112

Carolyn Watts: 98 (top), 119 (centre), 122 (top), 127 (top left)

Richard Webb Ltd: 23 (top)

Wheelock and Company Ltd: 67 (bottom), 90

Diane T. Woo: 69 (top)

Yau Leung: 61 (top left), 62 (top), 63 (top), 64, 72 (top), 73 (bottom), 74 (both), 84 (top, 89 (top), 123

Millie Yung: 31 (bottom)

Index

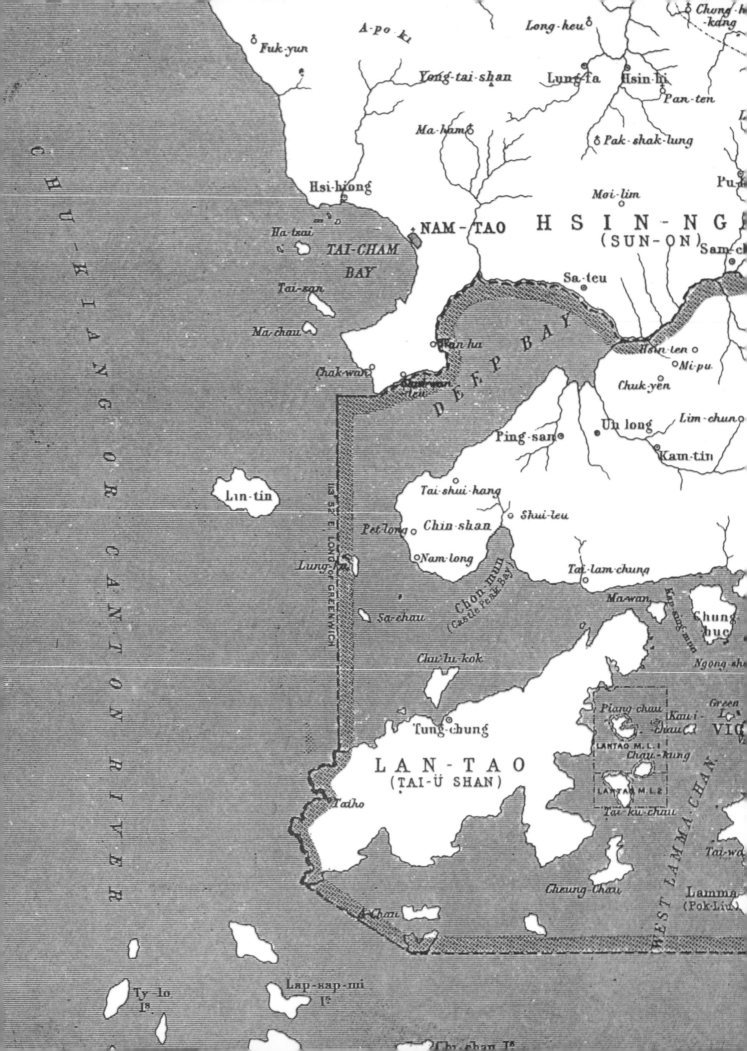

Fuk·yun

A·po·ki

Long·heu

Chung·ki
·kang

Yong·tai·shan   Lung·fa   Hsin·hi

Pan·ten

Ma·ham

Pak·shak·lung

Pu

Hsi·hiong

Moi·lim

NAM-TAO   HSIN-NG

(SUN-ON)

Sam·c

Ha·tsai

TAI-CHAM
BAY

Sa·teu

Tai·san

Wan·hu

DEEP BAY

Hsin·ten

Mi·pu

Ma·chau

Chak·wan   Shamuan
·teu

Chuk·yen

Lim·chun

Un·long

Ping·san

Kam·tin

Lin·tin

Tai·shui·hang

Shui·teu

Chin·shan

Pei·long

Nam·long

Tai·lam·chung

113° 52′ E. LONG. OF GREENWICH

Chon·mun
(Castle Peak Bay)

Ma·wan

Kap·sui·mun

Chung
·uc

Lung·ku

Sa·chau

Ngong·she

CHU·KIANG OR CANTON RIVER

Chu·lu·kok

Piang·chau   Kau·i·   Green
chau   L

LANTAO M.L.1

Chau·kung

VIC

Tung·chung

LANTAO M.L.2

LAN-TAO
(TAI-Ü SHAN)

Tai·ku·chau

Taiho

WEST LAMMA CHAN

Tai·wa

A·chau

Cheung·chau

Lamma
(Pok·Liu)

Ty·lo
I⁵.

Lap·sap·mi
I⁵.

Che·shan I⁵.